Inspiring Resilience

in Fearful

and Reactive Dogs

Sally Gutteridge

Copyright

No part of this book may be reproduced in any form - written, electronic, recording, or photocopying without written permission of the publisher or author. The exception would be in the case of brief quotations embodied in the critical articles or reviews and pages where permission is specifically granted by the author.

Although every precaution has been taken to verify the accuracy of the information contained herein, the author and publisher assume no responsibility for any errors or omissions. No liability is assumed for damages that may result from the use of information contained within.

Books may be purchased by contacting the publisher and author at:
info@sallygutteridge.com
www.sallygutteridge.com

Interior Layout: Sandeep Likhar
Editor: Rebecca Stranney
Illustrator: Dayle Smith

For Chips and all the dogs like him.

About the Author

Sally Gutteridge has been a full time educational writer since 2015 holding a variety of canine certifications. She is a former professional Dog Trainer with the Royal Army Veterinary Corps, former instructor with Hearing Dogs for Deaf People and has much rescue experience. Sally is a member of the Pet Professional Guild. She is a Graduate and award winner from The Writers Bureau. Through the organisation, Canine Principles, Sally along with a fantastic team, provides reputable Continuation of Professional Development for all canine professionals. Canine Principles teaches the most up to date, positive, scientific canine awareness.

Sally lives in Rural Cumbria with her ever patient husband and four rescued, cheeky terriers.

Table of Contents

Introduction

"Dogs are great. Bad dogs, if you can really call them that, are perhaps the greatest of them all." -John Grogan

The term 'reactive dog' is increasingly common. What it really means is that the dog who can't cope, overreacts. When we live with one of these dogs, they have our heart. We tend to have the ultimate patience for them and their erratic acts, sometimes way more patience than we have with the people in our lives. We work hard to make every moment of their lives a high-quality experience, we are even prepared to enter battle to protect them.

The dog that snuggles with us, wakes up with a squashed bottom lip and is pushed against our legs when we cry, that's the dog that we know. The defensive displays, barking, lunging and general hostility, that's the dog that others see.

Reaction is a behaviour. It's a response to certain triggers that defines one of your dog's personality traits. An overreaction is his way of coping with something that has made him feel threatened in some way. Your dog is not a reactive dog and his behaviour when stressed doesn't define him. Your dog is a loving, living animal that is bonded with you and looks to you as his friend and protector; just as he's your dog you are his human.

Your dog might be a playful dog, a friendly dog, a dog that learns quickly and that has taught himself words like "walk" or "dinner" but none of those things define him any more than the fact that sometimes he overreacts. Your dog is a living creature that does his best in the world that he has found himself in.

Resilience means strength and the ability to cope.

Resilience is a well-used term that encompasses many things but generally in dog terms means the ability to cope. Taken from the Latin term *resili* it means the ability to spring back from tension or testing conditions, with little damage. Physical resilience is seen in everything from the elastic band stretched to its limits then returning to its original shape, to the huge suspension bridge able to take the weight of many vehicles yet revert to its original form easily by design.

Emotional and psychological resilience for your dog is defined as the ability to remain flexible in emotional response or behaviour despite pressure from the environment, sometimes through long periods of time. Maintaining a good level of well-being and avoiding distress.

This book focuses on building your own awareness and knowledge, whilst simultaneously enhancing your dog's strength and ability to deal with situations he may find difficult. I will explain your dog's behaviour, give practical advice on positive change and help you to understand your dog better. Throughout our journey together your dog will become more resilient and your relationship with them will grow, your trust will deepen and together you will face a brighter world.

We begin our journey with focus on canine communication, stress in dogs and how behaviour occurs. We look at how dogs have evolved alongside us and the long-established relationship between the canine and human species.

We begin practical application by addressing the dog's basic right to have all their needs met and how we can help them to de-stress ready for positive change. We then move into practical behaviour change techniques and how they can be applied to empower the dog and build their resilience, enabling them to cope with stress triggers in everyday life. We then get practical, empowering you with a proven toolkit of knowledge and strategies, to understand and help the dog or dogs in your life. The overall aim of the book is to help dogs that may not be coping too well through the people closest to them, you.

Note: I refer to dogs in the book as "him" purely for ease of reading, the advice applies to males and females in equal measure.

Chapter One

"My little dog – a heartbeat at my feet."
– Edith Wharton

About Dogs

There are many myths about the domestic dog and why he does what he does. Fortunately, the dog that we live with now is also in the eye of science, we are learning more about the dogs we live with than we have ever known before. This gives us facts and findings to draw on when we are caring for, communicating and understanding dogs. Before we can look at any specific behaviour of a dog, we must first always consider who he is and where he came from.

Domestication is a human term, it means that we decide a species should live with us in some capacity and so make them domesticated. Some animals are domesticated for their bodies or what they can provide our appetites. They are farmed yet still wary of humans, maintaining the shy and inoffensive natures that made them easy to farm in the first place. Some are bred in boxes and sold as pets, often for children, whilst others joined us of partial free will and became our domesticated friends, work partners and amusers, including dogs.

Dogs have become a highly successful species in many ways, they share our homes, lives and hearts. They live in our homes with us, and become an integral member of the family.

There are a few different theories on how dogs and people became so close. The common one a few years ago was that we stole a few wolf cubs and made them our own. It now seems more likely that the dog is a descendent of the same ancestor of today's wild Gray Wolf and that they joined us because we were providers of food. Many animals we know today hang on to fringes of human settlements - driven by the availability of waste foods. Wolves may have been one of the earliest examples of this behaviour, which soon became co-operation between the tamest of their species and the most interested of ours.

Evolution Matters

As we have been able to explore DNA in greater detail thanks to scientific advances. We have moved on from relying on archaeological findings alone to learn how life on earth evolved via the availability of DNA of both early dogs and early humans.

DNA is the essence of our biological existence. Every single living thing has a totally unique genetic make-up, apart from identical twins. The genetic composition of any individual living creature is called their genome, this applies to us and to our dogs. The human genome is 25% identical to the genome of the domestic dog.

The dogs that live with us in our homes share most of their genetic inheritance with the wolf packs that live in the wild, up to 99% for many breeds. However, they share very little of their evolution with their wild cousins. We cannot assume therefore that dog and wolves are - and act - the same. Just as we can't assume that we will naturally act 25% dog, or that the dog in our life will act 25% human – we are very different animals.

A common theory on dog behaviour is that the dog is a wolf and will therefore act like a wolf in the home. Unfortunately, this idea has been perpetuated by the media and a few highly influential dog trainers. It's been further complicated by a misconception on how wild wolves act and why they act like they do.

Early studies of the Gray Wolf provided us with inaccurate results on the animal and how they naturally live and conduct themselves. Wolves in the wild live in family groups and generally do family things; they hunt, play, sleep and breed as a family. The mother and father are the only ones that produce cubs and the rest of the pack is extended family, usually made up of their cubs and sometimes siblings.

If we observe a pack of wolves in the wild, which we are now lucky enough to be able to do via excellent recording equipment and quiet observation from a distance, we see a tribal culture with its roots in family values. Wolves can appear quite overt in their inter-species communication; in comparison to family dogs. They can be vocal, appearing quite foreboding but that type of communication is perfectly natural for them and doesn't necessarily indicate conflict.

During 1947 at the Zoological Institute of the University of Basel in Switzerland; Robert Shenkel carried out one of the first observational studies on wolves, which also became one of the most influential studies on wolf behaviour for many years and in some cases is still referred to as justification for dog training methods today.

Schenkel presented his findings based on observation, with one very important omission, he failed to study wolves in their own natural environment or their own family group.

Early observation of natural wolf inter-species communication was attributed to problematic relationships within the wolf pack. The observation was also flawed as the wolves that were studied were unrelated as opposed to the natural dynamic of the wolf pack which we know of today. Whilst a family of wolves live together in peace, a group of unrelated wolves are unlikely to find peace in the same way, particularly as the animals had no choice over the other animals that they were penned in with. The close proximity increasing tension between the animals every time they were put into the environment; an environment which we can now consider overwhelming for them.

Schenkel presented a theory that wolves were in tension for their place in the group, which soon became considered a fact of life for this particular animal and transferred into advice for people that cared for and worked with the domestic dog. The observational scientist did his best with what he had and would likely have approached the study very differently in more recent times, sadly though the fact remains that his initial theory stuck with wolves and dogs; in many cases to this present day.

This has led to common dog training practices ranging from going through doors and eating before dogs, to physically manipulating them through force. None of which communicate our requirements to a dog in a language which he actually understands.

In the mid 1980's American Biologist David Mech carried out another famous study on wolf behaviour and began to notice the flaws in the earlier theory. Mech studied true wild wolves on Ellsmere Island Canada over a period of thirteen summers. He learned that a male and female wolf form the parents of a pack and lead the group into a hunt, because they are the most experienced. Mech also learned that the wild wolf pack is closer to a family nucleus than originally presented.

Domestication

Whilst we can explore wolf behaviour to dispel one of the most damaging myths of dog training and behaviour, we really cannot assume that dogs and wolves are the same animal at all. Domestication has led to the dog that we know today and in many ways, he is further removed from his Gray Wolf cousin than he has ever been before. So how did the split occur?

As we have already discussed, the dog's ancestor may have joined people as part of a quest for food. It is considered that the bolder animals would have been more likely to approach people whilst the shyer animals may have steered clear.

When animals are completely wild and reproduce naturally with no influence from humans their evolutional process is known as natural selection. The species grows and develops naturally during this type of evolution. The strongest animals usually breed whilst weak and sick animals don't, therefore the entire species becomes more robust.

When resources are plenty and every animal has safe access to food and freedom from predators, they tend to breed more frequently. This is because they have a security which keeps them safe and their bellies full. This is known as relaxed selection and is another type of evolution. The dogs that began to live around the settlements of early humans may have progressed into a period of relaxed selection because people produce plenty of resources, which we consider waste, but other animals can benefit from. This may have led to a boost in breeding. As each generation is born in safe circumstances, they will usually become bolder and more confident within those circumstances.

If we saw the bold animals as useful, which it seems we did, we would have then got involved in their evolution to benefit ourselves. This will have led to the ancestors of our dogs becoming our partners in many things - inclusive of hunting, finding food and physical work such as carrying packs or pulling sleds. At this point relaxed selection transitioned to early artificial selection. The act of artificial selection is the basis of all dog breeding at the hands of people – we choose the parents in the hope that they produce the kind of puppies we want. Early in the evolutionary process of the domestic dog, people are likely to have wanted stronger fighters, faster hunters and the most useful animals and so bred from the stronger parents to produce more useful offspring.

Artificial selection, with a dash of environmental influence, created all the dog breeds that we know today.

The difference of appearance depends on a number of things including the environment the dog originally lived in. An Alaskan Malamute for example has a thick coat, to keep him warm in the freezing environments that he originally lived and because his initial artificial selection took place in that environment his coat will have naturally stayed the same.

In the Nineteenth Century, dog showing and sports became popular. This led to a boost in artificial selection which wasn't determined by the use of dogs for basic survival. With human travel and the ability to move breed types around the globe, we began to see the start of multi breed shows and pet dogs from all over the world.

Dog breeding became a profession. Hunters bred from their strongest dogs and sold working breeds to other hunters, show enthusiasts bred dogs suitable for show and this continued right to the present day. Various kennel clubs were founded, who presented a set of breed standards that they used as guidelines for breeding and showing dogs. A practice that is still current but criticised by various welfare organisations, as dictated appearance affects health in many cases.

Current dog breeders include; hobby breeders that breed in their homes, people that breed dogs with care and attention and do it ethically, accidental and backyard breeders and a large amount of puppy farmers that breed hundreds of puppies for selling to pet homes through classifieds, every week. Puppy farms are usually large scale breeding operations, where welfare is second to profit. These organisations are licenced by local councils and dogs usually live in barns or kennels.

Everything about how and why they are bred will affect the wellbeing of a dog. From the moment they are conceived, or to be more accurate, from the moment their ancestors are conceived.

Responsible breeders are more likely to create puppies that are physically, socially, emotionally and psychologically sound. However, responsible dog breeding is a lifestyle and full-time job. Meeting all the needs of parent dogs and new born puppies, to ensure they are ready to go to a new home, is time consuming and a labour of love. Puppy farmers do very little to care for parents and puppies before they sell them on, so they meet only the basic needs to keep the breeding dogs and their puppies alive long enough to keep the cash flowing, and there are many more farmed dogs than responsibly bred dogs.

Considering the ratio of responsible breeders to the other types mentioned above, we are more often seeing dogs that suffer from irresponsible breeder selection than we see sound and confident puppies. It's easy to buy a puppy from a puppy farm, that has already learned the world is a scary place and has physical and psychological health issues by the time they are a few weeks old. This current availability of puppies from classifieds, pet stores and newspapers has developed over the last two or three decades, and the last five years or so has seen a rise in worried, fearful and non-resilient dogs.

It's important to note here that dogs are as individual as people. We can't offer a blanket approach for their behaviour as a species – or as a single dog. We simply gain the best understanding we can of the species in their entirety, then we observe an individual dog to work out the personal reasons for their actions along with how we can best help them.

The development of any animal, inclusive of humans is dictated by the environment that the animal is born into. So, a dog that is conceived in a stressful environment and develops whilst their mother is stressed will usually be prepared for a stressful world before they are born. Add to this the genetic influence of the dog's parents and prior ancestors and we start to see the development of a dog's nature, well before it's shown in their behaviour.

Breeding a dog, via artificial selection, for a specific purpose will usually affect the way that dog behaves on a basic level. The Border Collie, with his long line of herding ancestors, shows specific behaviours associated with finely tuned herding and working traits. These are biological factors that naturally affect his behaviour.

Most dog breeds were tuned via artificial selection for a purpose. Labradors were bred to fetch game birds that have been shot from the sky. Spaniels have been bred to do that and flush the same birds into the sky. The terrier was bred to dig, catch and shake small animals, whilst a Shih Tzu has been bred specifically as a companion dog, leaving him particularly easy to care for in a family home when carefully bred and nurtured from conception.

All dogs will have biological factors to their behaviour. Sometimes it's obvious to see, whilst at other times it's diluted and confused, for example the Cavalier King Charles spaniel who chases birds for fun or the terrier that chases cats in the street but will happily tolerate or even befriend a cat in their home.

Every generation of dog that is born will be a tiny bit closer to being suitable for the environment that they will occupy. It is often not a recognisable change within one or two generations but it's a natural process for a dog to be born a little readier to survive in their current environment. This preparation can work to increase or decrease a dog's capacity for the role which he is being prepared.

An example of increased capacity is the Sighthound's sharp eyesight that allows them to spot a rabbit's slightest movement in the distance, or the Border Collie's eyesight being so sharp that it can spot a stray sheep in low light following the smallest movement at great distance.

An example of decreased capacity is the puppy farmed dog that is born in a dark environment then kept there to be bred from – in the same environment – who doesn't fully develop eyesight or hearing because neither of them are really needed. After a few years in a puppy farm, our own little Yorkie shows greatly diminished eyesight which could show us that she is likely to have been there since she was born. She also has total intolerance to grass, which may show that she has never been near it long enough to build up a tolerance, therefore contact with grass makes her itchy.

There have been a number of studies focussed on the changes that can occur to DNA after an animal is born. Whilst we are aware that DNA is set soon after conception, scientists have recently found that it can be affected by an area known as epigenetics. The term epigenome means "above the genome" which we already know is the dog's full genetic code, his DNA. The epigenome cannot change the dog's DNA, but it can decide which parts of the dog's genome are needed in their current environment – to best benefit the dog. So, whilst the genome can't be affected by the environment, it can be switched on or off in the most useful places by the epigenome. If a genetic trait is switched off for long enough, the DNA of a new puppy may not inherit the trait at all. This is in part why evolution can change a species, animal by animal, via their passing on of DNA.

Environmental Influence

Whilst we have so far considered the biological aspects that form a dog's personality and behaviour, we must also consider how the environment helps to shape them into who they are. A puppy that is born into a loving home and learns to trust all other living animals – including people- in that home will become quite a trusting dog. The term given to learning is conditioning and a dog that learns they are safe will usually assume they are safe unless something or someone shows them otherwise.

Sometimes pregnant mother dogs are rescued from highly stressful conditions and their puppies have already started to develop ready for a stressful world. Yet if that puppy meets security and the puppy learns from birth that he's safe, he will have an excellent chance of growing into a capable and confident dog.

If a perfectly bred puppy, to confident parents, is homed into abusive circumstances that puppy may learn fear very early in his young life, leading to a stressed and anxious older dog.

In addition, a puppy can learn to fear something that we see as perfectly normal, and this may affect him throughout his entire life in a process that we refer to as 'one trial learning'. An example of one trial learning would be being stuck in a strange house with a fire alarm going off, at a sensitive age and then being scared of the house forever.

When an individual dog meets certain circumstances, either an ability to cope, or a tendency to become stressed, is formed. Just as it is with children and even adults if the circumstances and emotional response aligns in a way that enables such a response. Our role is to fully assess the dog or dogs in our care and find out if they cope, and if they don't cope what we can do to make their lives easier, empower them and build their ability to be resilient in their everyday lives.

Man's Best Friend

The dogs that we know today are the result of at least hundreds of years of domestication. This means that they have not only evolved separately from their wild ancestors but that they have evolved living closely to the human species. This close proximity to people has led to a fully domesticated dog that understands and communicates with the human species with skill, competence and an impressive social ability.

In some ways the domestic dog's ability to communicate with humans has led to a reliance on us. A recent study compared the domestic dog's ability to carry out teamwork with another dog, to the capacity for teamwork between wolves. The dogs were found to be less capable.

There are many tests and studies showing us exactly how dogs and humans co-operate in everything from everyday life to the bonding of our two species.

Whilst we speak a different language to the dogs that we live with, they have taught themselves our intentions, by reading our expressions and micro-expressions. Dogs have perfected left gaze bias all on their own. The dog will read the micro expressions associated with human emotions on their human's face, at exactly the time the same emotions are recognised in the brain on the opposite side, because the dog looks to our left, the practice has been termed left gaze bias.

In return humans have made little effort, as a whole, to fully understand the requests and communication attempts of our dogs. We learn the small signals and requests by conscious effort, but generally we assume we know how a dog feels by projecting our opinions onto him. Thankfully we now live in an age of information, where we can learn about general dog behaviour and communication then apply that knowledge to better understand the dogs in our lives.

Takeaway Points

- The idea that wolves strive for dominance in a natural pack is based on a study that has since been disproven.
- Wolves live in a family pack and co-operate to ensure survival of the group.
- Whilst dogs and wolves share most of their DNA they have evolved differently which will affect their behaviour in every area of their respective lives.
- Dogs usually live in a multi-species family group which includes humans.
- Not all dogs get a good start in life and this can affect their well-being and behaviour throughout their lives.
- Environmental factors can affect a dog's ability to cope or become stressed in any situation.
- The behaviour of any individual dog is a unique mix of his biology, learning experiences and the environment which he finds himself in.
- Our role as dog guardians is to help the dogs in our care to become empowered and resilient to stress, by promotion of positive behaviours and encouraging well-being.

Chapter Two

"If dogs could talk, perhaps we would find it as hard to get along with them as we do with people." – Capek

Canine Behaviour

To fully understand canine reactions and how we can help a dog that is struggling with life - enough to be regularly reactive to things in his immediate environment - we must first understand the basics of behavioural science.

The study of behaviour has been carried out for a long time. Just as we study the behaviour of dogs, we spend a lot of time exploring the behaviour of people. In fact, there is an entire – human based – psychology practice focused on behaviourism and it's essentially parallel to the study of behaviour in dogs.

Canine behaviour is defined as an external display of an internal state. If a dog is scared on the inside, they will show it on the outside and that display gives us clues as to how the dog feels. The more we know about dog body language, the better we can help the dog. Generally, if we see a behaviour change in a dog – we can usually see the external stimulus that triggered the change. This external stimulus then impacts the dog's emotional state.

Important note: Not all behaviours will have obvious external triggers. Pain and biological changes for example will often impact behaviour. We will observe this behaviour change but not the internal trigger. This is one of the reasons we must always consider a veterinary assessment when a dog's behaviour changes suddenly.

Canine behaviour is fascinating. The study of an animal's behaviour in their natural environment is known as ethology. With dogs, this study is made possible and highly popular due to domestication and their evolution to consider our homes as their natural environment. Every single dog guardian and professional can be an ethologist, by observing, studying and learning about dog behaviour from the dogs in our care. Add to this a healthy interest in the studies carried out by scientists in all fields over the last few years and we can become very well informed on the internal state of our dogs; simply because they are telling us via their behaviour!

Not only does the study of behaviour tell us how a dog is feeling but it also tells us the best way to change how a dog feels about those things which cause him stress and fear. With even the smallest application of behavioural science, we can build a dog's resilience and ability to cope, beyond the stress and fear that he has learned in his life so far.

There are a lot of complex terms about learning theory, behaviour and how a consequence will affect a future act. They can be a little overwhelming but are all important, so we will tackle them gradually, leaving you with a new understanding by the end of this book.

Reactive Behaviour

Reactive behaviour is a sign that the internal state of the dog has changed and that the dog is dog suffering with an emotion such as stress, fear, frustration or anxiety.

It is strictly speaking, an overreaction and can include lunging, barking, threatening or trying to get away. The exact behaviour type and reason for it will depend on the dog, their personality and capacity to cope. We will discuss exact communication and what it means in the next chapter.

Whilst overt overreaction is obvious, the other response is less obvious and can be completely missed by the untrained eye, yet it is still a reaction – a response to a changed internal state. A dog that doesn't display their feelings by trying to scare the other dog away, or even offering an aggressive display, will be less noticeable and can even look happy or considered 'well-behaved'. The dog that suffers emotional 'shut-down' during a reaction is why we most often hear from dog guardians that their dog is reactive by being difficult to handle and in an overtly wound up and aggressive state.

Another misconception about a specific dog reaction is the dog that shows barrier frustration. Most often displayed from the dog that's on a lead, barking through a fence or behind a gate, barrier frustration is the result of a physical barrier that prevents interaction. Whilst barrier frustration can certainly become aggression if not dealt with carefully, it can be addressed early on by changing the environment and consequences of a behaviour to dissipate and then prevent the over-arousal associated with the object of the dog's attention.

Over and hyper-arousal is a dog behaviour that we most often see from a dog that is stressed and overwhelmed. This behaviour is caused by the dog's inability to be calm and relaxed. It's fundamentally a sign of excess mental and physical energy, over-stimulation and an influx of stress hormones that doesn't dissipate as it should. Often a dog that is hyper-aroused will jump up, they may nip hands and they cannot read the social requests of other dogs so are socially incompetent in their well-meaning but misled desperation to interact with their own species. The hyper-aroused dog is difficult to handle on a lead and in the care of an inexperienced handler can be accused of bad or naughty behaviour. The idea that this behaviour is voluntary can lead to human frustration or even punishment, from the guardian or uneducated trainer, which will make the dog even more stressed.

Sometimes we see the hyper-aroused dog forced into perceived calmness via threats or punishment; by someone that may be considered a strong trainer showing their dominance. This unacceptable behaviour hasn't dealt with the dog's feelings, it has made the dog too intimidated to show them, but the internal turmoil will show in another way at some point.

The only true way to help a stressed dog is to help them to decompress by ensuring their needs are met, teaching them to be calm, empowering them via positive behaviour modification and building their natural personal resilience in the long term.

Stress

Stress is an internal reaction. It is an innate response to a threat and leads to a number of changes within the body.

There is variation in the types of stress that a dog may experience and sometimes it's effective and helpful. A dog that is learning something new for example, may experience a surge of positive stress known as Eustress. This brief release of stress hormones enables peak performance. If a dog is just about to learn something and is on the edge of getting worried - they may briefly experience this helpful stress – that gives their mind a eureka moment. This is followed by the reward of success for the dog and possibly a coaching reward from their owner.

Other types of stress may not be helpful i.e. stress that is detrimental to the well-being of a dog. Similar to people, if a dog's needs are not met sufficiently in all areas, they will be susceptible to stress. Any dog that suffers from hunger, social deprivation, emotional turmoil or a feeling of being unsafe, on a regular basis, will probably suffer from stress. This is particularly so if the dog hasn't built resilience, or has deep set anxiety issues.

The two types of stress that can be damaging to dogs are known as short-term or long-term stress. Short term stress is an acute, sudden stress response, long term is when that stress response is ongoing, and the dog never gets a chance to relax or recover before the body is releasing more stress hormones.

The physical changes that occur when a dog gets stressed take place their nervous system. The survival response begins, and the dog is subjected to a physical and psychological need to fight, freeze or take flight. This is an ancient response that we as humans also experience at some point. It's an innate, ingrained instinctive response to anything we consider a potential threat to our safety and survival.

In the case of our dogs, who live in a world dictated by us and all things human, it can become more acute due to lack of choice. Dogs live in our world, with cars, fireworks, noise, screaming babies and household appliances even when they don't understand these things. The dog has no choice but to be in the park near a toddler that might grab them at any time. They can't escape the sound of fireworks for four weeks either side of a public holiday and they don't instinctively know that the postman isn't going to harm everyone in the home at the first opportunity. In short, by living with us, the ability of our dogs to have choices in their lives is greatly diminished and the potential for stress increased.

Even when we try our level best to offer choices to our dogs, we are still very much in charge of their lives. We tell them when and what they eat, when they go out and where they go – we can ask them but as they can't respond that well it's still in part guesswork on our part. We decide who our dogs meet, who they walk passed without greeting and we decide when to play with them or teach them something new. All of these things are offered with the best intentions, because none of us want bored, unhappy, badly fed and under exercised dogs.

We naturally want the best for our dogs, often at the expense of our own life quality; but the fact remains that we are in charge of their lives. In many ways this suits them perfectly. They share the best seats and beds in the house, they eat well and get plenty of attention. The lucky ones get walks in many different areas, coaching and enrichment. Their health is managed, and they get plenty of love, so it's not all dictators and prison. For most dogs, domestication has worked out very well indeed.

However;

Sometimes a dog doesn't feel like they can cope with a situation or an environment and that makes them stressed. Stress then changes their internal state and the result is a change to their behaviour.

Stress Triggers.

Anything that causes a dog stress is known as a trigger. There are other terms, but for clarity throughout this book we will refer to a trigger. The trigger is unique to the dog, some dogs cope really well with strangers whilst others find them terrifying. The reason for the trigger is part of the dog's individuality. The underlying reason for a stress response may be something physical, such as a genetically inherited fear or he may have learned the fear from another dog or from a scary past experience.

Overreacting due to exposure to triggers is physically and psychologically damaging and will eventually lead to ill health. In addition, a dog that has suffered a stressful experience and been exposed to a trigger continues to experience the physical reaction even when the trigger is removed. It can take up to 72 hours for a dog to return to a base state of calm after exposure to a particularly strong trigger.

If a dog has repeated or long-term exposure to stress triggers and reacts regularly with fear or defensive displays, their long term physical and mental health will suffer. When a dog believes they are in danger their body switches immunity and digestion to a lesser important function, which if occurs regularly can cause problems within the body.

Energy that the body previously allocated to the immune system is rerouted to prepare the dog for the perceived imminent threat, and the fight, flight, or freeze response. Whilst the stressor(s) remain present, the dog's immune system doesn't get the chance to return to normal and to do its job of protecting the dog.

A dog enduring long-term stress, will be more likely to be affected by disease and illness, and will take longer to recover from these and from any injuries due to the suppression of the normal bodily responses.

Another impact of long-term stress is a depressed digestion capacity. As the body is regularly flooded with stress chemicals which tell it that, at any moment, the dog may need to fight or flee so a stomach full of undigested food must be avoided. Any reduction of food digestion will mean a lower calorific intake, so the dog will have less energy. That means he may appear listless and tired so may try to sleep more but, being stressed, will likely find sleep elusive as he's constantly on edge, and fearful of what's around. The reduction in food consumption will mean fewer nutrients being available for absorption by the cells in the dog's body which, in turn, means they'll be less able to regenerate to replace decaying cells.

A dog under stress will also have higher levels of emotion-related hormones and these will be repeatedly triggered every time the dog is exposed to his stressors. This recurring hormone production will put even greater pressure on the already suppressed immune system and can leave the dog's body in something of a vicious cycle. The dog is stressed so his immune system is suppressed so he's more vulnerable to illness which, if illness does strike, means he's less able to fight it off, making him feel unwell, which leads to them feeling more stressed.

All these physical changes happen when our dogs overreact regularly enough to cause long-term stress.

Trigger Stacking

Trigger stacking is the process of meeting a lot of triggers in a short amount of time, to the point that the dog can no longer cope at all.

Without the opportunity to calm between scary experiences a dog's stress levels will continue to rise. The point where a dog can no longer cope is called his coping threshold. You may hear or have read the term threshold before, it basically means a dog's breaking point. Sometimes a dog will react quickly and to one scary experience, whilst at other times he will stay below his threshold and achieve enough space and time to recover, so he never reacts. But once a dog has reached his threshold he is likely to react to all triggers until he is given the opportunity to calm down, over as long as 72 hours.

When a dog has a poor ability to cope with triggers in the environment and we can manage those triggers. We can keep the dog below threshold by managing our dog's safe space and increasing distance between our dog and his triggers. If a trigger enters a dog's safe space without warning, and sends the dog over their coping threshold, the dog is then likely to become hyper-alert and likely to react more quickly for the next few hours.

A real-life example is this. A dog that is scared of children may cope with a child ten meters away at the park, playing quietly (trigger 1). If the distance stays the same but the child begins to scream (trigger 2), the dog may not cope as screaming has added a second trigger and the entire thing has naturally become a scarier scenario, so the dog may bark. However, if the dog can cope with the screaming and stays under their threshold but then another screaming child runs in (trigger 3) that might be just too much for the dog and he will go over threshold and react.

If the dog is really resilient despite his fear of children, he may cope with these three triggers at a safe distance; but if a third child appeared a little closer, the dog may go over his threshold and react.

These triggers don't need to be related at all. A dog who is scared of unknown people may walk by three strangers and react on the fourth. Not because there is something particularly scary about stranger number four but because four strangers are all the triggers he can take in the short amount of time that he met them. When we have this knowledge; we start to get a much better understanding of what our dogs are experiencing when they are out in the world. The point that they react to something is not random. The reason is always there - if we look carefully and learn to read our dogs, we will be able to see it.

Trigger stacking is often the reason that a dog may bite. He can cope with things on some days, when he is generally relaxed, but on other days, maybe after a few scary experiences, he may not be able to cope with exactly the same thing. A dog on a TV chat show for example, may never have bitten anyone in his life but add the light, acoustics, heat, chaos and smells to a presenter that forces a hand or face into the dog's safe space and we have a trigger stacked dog that goes over threshold, simply because he can't cope anymore. This may lead to the dog biting the TV presenter.

We could have a calm dog leaving the house, but then we go to the vets. We leave the vets and pass a noisy digger on the way to the park and a few minutes later a storm blows in. Until now our dog has coped remarkably well, then a stranger tries to talk to him. We lose our opportunity to increase distance between our dog and this final trigger; the dog goes over threshold and reacts. We then spend the rest of the walk dealing with a dog that is over threshold and simply can't cope with any trigger that he sees.

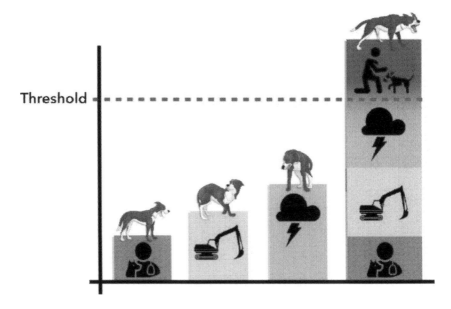

If this happens on every walk the dog will soon start to anticipate fear as he leaves the house and may be ready to go over threshold early in the walk. Or we may have a few excellent walks where the dog is relaxed and never goes over threshold, only to be hit with a bunch of inescapable triggers. These cause the dog enough stress to go over his threshold.

When we empower the dog through canine coaching and build his resilience, the threshold to cope gets higher and the dog is generally less susceptible to stress.

Understanding and Changing Behaviour

Understanding how behaviour works is associated with creating positive change. The first thing we must acknowledge when planning to work with the behaviour of a dog is that behavioural science is based in facts. A number of well-known names are associated with many studies on behaviour and how it is learned and repeated by any organism that finds it beneficial. People and dogs both repeat things that we find rewarding. Any consequence of behaviour will drive us to repeat that behaviour time and again.

An example of this in people is addiction. If you drink a cup of strong coffee in a morning before beginning your day, you are likely to experience a caffeine buzz. That influx of stimulant will make the day seem easier, by giving you energy that you didn't have before the coffee kicked in. Drinking the coffee has provided you with a reward, a change in the way you feel therefore, tomorrow morning you will most likely switch the coffee machine on before you do anything else. Before you know it, you have an addiction caused by the consequence of that first cup of coffee.

People and dogs both have a reward centre in our brain, its basis is a neurotransmitter called Dopamine. When something happens that we like, Dopamine is produced in the brain and it feels great. This particular neurotransmitter is also associated with memory and motivation, so in short it feels good, or at least feels rewarding, and we associate what we were doing at the time with that feeling and try it again in the future.

For our dogs, Dopamine is an excellent coaching tool. It helps dogs learn, plus be motivated and happy whilst they learn. It can also drive repeated behaviour that we would prefer didn't exist, because a dog will always choose their own rewards. An example of this is the dog that chases away the postman. The fact that the stranger is leaving is linked to the dog's own defensive display and their noisy barking is rewarded by a hasty retreat of the scary stranger.

There are a few key points of canine behaviour. They are definite points that will always occur and in essence they are quite simple. The complexity comes from individuality but can be solved by observation and education, though the following points will remain the same:

A display of behaviour is always indicative of an internal state. So, the dog feels a certain way and the way that he is acting is because of how he feels.

Something will always happen before a behaviour change. It may be something extremely simple such as eye contact or a trigger in the distance, or it may be complex like an internal pain or subtle association. Either way it will always occur and if we are careful and generous with our observations we can recognise the change that preludes behaviour change.

The behaviour that is displayed will be determined by the individual dog. It may be a learned, habitual or stress driven response. The behaviour may be similar between dogs; which it obviously is considering the rise in defensive acts and behaviours that we consider reaction and over-reaction. A dog may have learned that they are helpless in unknown situations, so they shut down, or they may have learned that antagonistic acts get them the space they desperately want. The behaviour may be habitual, or the stress could be so severe that the dog is always over threshold. Whatever the individual response, we must always look to the dog to learn the reason for it.

A consequence will always drive repeated behaviour. So, the dog that finds a consequence to be rewarding is likely to repeat the behaviour that they have naturally associated with the consequence. Like chasing away the delivery guy, it worked and achieved their aim, so they repeat it next time someone appears at the entrance to their home.

If we change the consequence with skill, care and kindness, we can naturally change the behaviour. For this to be truly effective we must first remove any negative stress and anxiety from the situation, via careful exposure at a pace with which the dog can cope.

Dogs will always define and decide upon their own reward and motivators. Just as we cannot successfully project how we think a dog feels onto how they actually feel, we cannot decide what a dog finds rewarding or motivating. We can help them along by working out what they like and what motivates them, and supplying this at the right time. Ultimately though, they get to decide their reward. Which is just how it should be – for their sake and for the best possible ease of learning something new.

When we know the dog's motivators and preferred rewards we can use them as consequences of behaviour. We can set up scenarios where the dog succeeds, this will in part empower them and naturally build their resilience and motivation to offer changed behaviours.

Whilst the above points show the fundamental knowledge of how we can change behaviours, with dogs that suffer from stress and have a number of stress triggers we can't just go ahead and attempt behaviour change. We must first work out what stresses them, how stressed they are and what they are trying to tell us via a process of effective canine communication. When we can read our dogs, we are better placed to help them.

Takeaway Points

- A dog's behaviour is an external display of his internal state. How a dog acts will tell us how he feels.
- Reactive behaviour is linked to an internal state of stress.
- The dog's exact behavioural response to stress will depend on their individuality.
- Stress is usually triggered by something in the dog's environment.
- Triggers can stack up; causing the dog to suffer extreme stress that goes above his ability to cope. The dog that reacts has usually gone over his coping threshold.
- A dog's response to stress triggers can be changed but the stress must be addressed first.
- Changing the dog's ability to cope will raise the dog's stress threshold and is called behaviour modification. This can be achieved by well-managed exposure to triggers - at the dog's pace - along with careful use of motivators, rewards and consequences.
- Behaviour modification will empower the dog that shows reactive behaviour, it will also build their resilience and make them less likely to suffer from regular stress.

Chapter Three

"Dogs do speak, but only to those who know how to listen."- Orhan Pamuk

Canine Communication

The way that our dogs communicate with us and each other is the foundation of all positive change. As dog guardians and professionals, we have an important role; we help dogs to live in the world we place them in and do our level best to make it a pleasant experience for them. Sadly, in many cases people still misinterpret the most important requests or communication attempts that dogs offer. There are many self-appointed professionals that misrepresent dogs too, based on their own misunderstanding of the domestic dog. That said, excellent and open-minded dog people have learned enough over the last few years, to truly understand much of the truth behind canine communication. It is the truth of the matter that we will discuss here.

It's vital to remember the following points and recognise their place in canine communication for the individual dog;

The communication attempts of dogs are affected by how they look and what they have learned. A dog that shows a default 'fight' response towards triggers has learned that response, usually by associating it with a motivational reward – remember that the dog decides their reward and a retreating trigger (scary threat) for a frightened dog is a perfect life reward.

A dog's accent is often decided by their breed type and physical appearance. This is particularly relevant for dogs that have been physically altered for aesthetic reasons: for example docked tails, long facial and body hair or a particularly muscular appearance which naturally appears as posturing.

Add the points above to a scenario, include a hearty dose of observation along with knowledge of innate canine communication and you can get an excellent idea of a dog's individual stress triggers and the basis for reactive behaviour in an individual dog.

Social Competence

Just like people, all dogs have their own social competence. Some are socially excellent, but others struggle to understand their own species. The dog that has an inability to communicate with other dogs is usually a result of poor social learning, or stressful experiences around others as they developed from puppy to adult.

Any dog that is deprived of adequate positive social learning with other dogs – for the first few months of their life - is likely to be awkward around other dogs forever.

A dog that is attacked will learn that other dogs are a threat. This is especially relevant if the attacked dog is young and passing through a critical learning period, but any scary experience can become a crippling associated fear if it's severe enough.

A dog that suffers at the hands of people is likely to have trust issues with people. Isolation or inexperience of people can cause fear of humans too, we often see this when dogs meet young children for the first time as adolescents or adults. They find the noise and movements of young children intimidating or worrying – not because they have been hurt by them – just because they don't understand them.

A dog that spends the first few months of their life learning excellent social awareness and communication, but is then isolated, will regress socially.

In addition, if a puppy learns their social skills from a socially competent adult dog that puppy is likely to grow up socially competent too.

Or if the adult role model is anxious or reactive, the puppy will usually learn to be worried too – resulting in two reactive dogs as opposed to one.

Poor social competence is the basis of reactive behaviour which is directed towards other dogs or people. The dog that sees another dog and launches into a tirade of noisy threats, is simply coping in a way that they believe will keep them safe. They usually haven't got the ability to defend themselves, so they are telling the other dog to stay away by being as loud and off putting as they can.

All dogs have a timeline of genetic inheritance and learning experiences which makes them who they are. Sometimes we know details of this and often we don't. The good news is that whilst details help understanding, we don't need them when we decide to execute positive change. All we need to help our dogs, are enlightened observation and intelligent education.

Learning about canine communication is your golden ticket to enlightened observation.

Enlightened Observation

Observation of any dog will give us an idea of how the dog is feeling, what the dog is saying and what in the environment is affecting them. All three of these things are crucial understanding for all successful communication but in a dog that tends to be reactive, they are extra important.

When learning about the communication of an individual dog the first thing to do is assess and learn to recognise their neutral state. Neutral body language is the essence of a relaxed dog. The neutral stance includes relaxed ears, facial expression and tail position. There is no posturing for a relaxed dog, they are comfortable and confident enough to *just be.*

Remember that breed dictates individuality. So, whilst a whippet's tail may tuck under their back legs as neutral position, the Spitz tail in the same position will show fear, unease or severe stress. It's advisable to research the dog's breed a little, inclusive of their natural, neutral stance in order to be fully informed when initially getting to know a dog via observation.

From the neutral stance, which is a relaxed dog, the body language will change depending on how a dog's feelings change. For example, feeding time may make the dog happy and excited which results in soft, flowing movements and the body language of anticipation. In the case of the relaxed dog that experiences a stress trigger, the body language will change in a very different way.

Greetings

A successful greeting between dogs is short and perfectly communicated. Eye contact is avoided, and scent has an important role. If both dogs are socially competent, they will curve around and aim for each other's information packed anal glands, have a sniff and choose to either interact further or agree to move on.

Dogs generally size each other up for greeting well before they get close enough to touch. There is a lot of distance communication which may involve meta signals such as lip licking, glancing away or blinking. All the signals are easily missed by the human eye, unless you are practicing enlightened observation.

The bigger dog in this picture is the more confident of the two, look at his tail, posture and focus. The smaller dog is unsure as his tail is lower, ears pulled back and his lips show tension. As a snapshot in time there is much communication occurring here.

Whilst we may miss this subtle 'I mean no harm' communication, socially competent dogs will not. The dog in the picture below shows a big lip and nose lick, which is a communication and calming gesture.

Off lead greetings are healthiest as being on the lead adds an odd dynamic to the situation. However, dogs should only be off lead to greet if both dogs are happy and both guardians have given permission. An on-lead greeting can cause tension and should be avoided if possible, or kept short, with a quick progress to a side by side walk or parting of ways within one or two seconds of the initial contact.

A dog that shows a hard eyed stare will most often do so with an on lead greeting. Staring is a prelude to a more overt behaviour so it's important to change the situation if one dog is staring at another.

One dog in this picture is uneasy, the other is staring. Look at the eyes on the left and the lip lick on the right, along with the reluctance to meet the staring dog's gaze.

The dog in the middle of this group looks vulnerable - see how his body is tucked. He's not meeting the other dogs' eyes even though they are both staring at him.

When happy and competent dogs greet a new dog, they first establish communications then they initiate the next step. Sometimes this is play and at other times it's a goodbye. The exact scenario will depend on the dogs.

Play is initiated by animated behaviour including a play bow and small jumps plus a relaxed play face - with soft eyes and a relaxed mouth. In this picture the terrier is trying hard to play and the spaniel is a little worried by his advances, note the lip lick.

A dog that is happy in this scenario will mirror the soft body language, they may show excitement and a willingness to play by returning the play bow and maintaining a play face expression of their own.

The next two pictures show dogs with play faces. They are characterised by wide mouths, squinty eyes and ears pulled back. This dog will have relaxed or excited body language.

Here's a play bow that says "throw the ball"

It's vital that both dogs are happy with any prolonged interaction. Part of the social incompetence that we have nurtured in many domestic dogs is the inability to read or respect other dogs. If one dog is determined to play and the other is scared or stressed, the scenario needs to be brought under control immediately. When a dog is trying to play with a scared dog they often chase and pounce on the terrified animal and this causes a great deal of stress for the victim.

This scenario is one of the biggest problems for guardians of fearful or reactive dogs. Unfortunately, it is too common and often something that cannot easily be controlled in the environments that are available to us for dog walks. Many people free run their dogs and fail to recall them or prevent their disruptive behaviour, so we end up backed into a corner with a stressed dog and nowhere to go. This is why we can relate so well with each other and choose our walk times and environments carefully. It's also the reason that we can't just avoid the problem and need to help our dogs to become resilient enough to cope with environmental factors that are naturally beyond our control.

Mild Signs of Stress

A dog that is tense or worried about a greeting will show that tension in his own body language and stance. This is the point that the dog may be experiencing the onset of the stress reaction that we discussed earlier. Mild anxiety may become stress then fear.

Signs of mild anxiety in a dog may include the following;

- Body or facial tension.
- Ears pulled back to the top of, or held out at the sides of the head.
- Head dipping below the other dog's face or below the dog's spine and shoulder height.
- Licking the lips or nose.
- Lips pulled in and back, showing a tense mouth.
- Looking or glancing away into the distance.
- Lowered tail from neutral position.
- One paw lifted. This is a position used for a variety of communication and should be observed in context with the other signs.
- Shaking as if removing water from the coat after leaving a pool or bath.
- Sniffing the ground in an attempt to defuse the situation and pretend it's not really happening.
- Trying to avoid eye contact and interaction, this is sometimes interpreted as ignoring by the unenlightened observer.
- Yawning.

Any socially competent dog will read these signs and respectfully leave the uneasy dog alone.

A human enlightened observer will also remove their attention from the dog who shows one or more of these signs, providing the dog with the space which they obviously need.

Later when we begin the practical coaching, we will reaffirm that these signs are the most important first signal - we need to read them and act upon them in order to execute positive change.

Appeasement

In some cases, when scared of the other dog or human a dog will display appeasement behaviour which is specifically used to communicate their unwillingness to engage in conflict with the person or animal that they are interacting with. This appeasement behaviour usually appears to prevent the onset of conflict and to pacify the other party. The types of acts included in appeasement are lip licking, tail wagging low and fast, pawing, lowered posture and ears pulled back. The dog may roll over or lift one paw, younger dogs may urinate. We could consider appeasement behaviour as a fearful dog outwardly announcing their fear or anxiety to anyone they are interacting with.

Dominance and Submission

Dominance and submission are descriptive terms that should ideally only be applied to the interactions and relationships formed between dogs. Dominance does exist but as a snippet in time, or as part of a bigger interaction and always between dogs or as part of canine communication. Dominant does not define a personality but a role. We should strive to avoid the use of the term when describing the relationship between dogs and people.

When dogs meet for the first time they may adopt a dominant or submissive role. Even bonded dogs may show dominance over a resource they particularly value, via resource guarding. In essence though, dominance is fluid and really depends on which dog is stronger in any unique situation or simply which dog is willing to go furthest to keep a resource.

The term alpha is often related to dominance, in reality alpha simply means the animals in a group that are able to breed. For example the mother and father wolf of a wild family pack are the alphas because they are the breeding pair and the rest of the family are their offspring. If one of their adult cubs begins to breed they will usually form a different family group of their own, which results in a new pack.

Dominance and submission is usually peaceful. On meeting, one dog may appear confident, triggering a less confident dog to defer and show subtle submissive signals that keep the peace. One dog may hold a resource in high importance whilst another may defer to them, because the resource is less important to them or they simply don't want to do battle for it.

Another thing to remember about dominance and the domestic dog is their evolution alongside humans. The ability to mate, eat and take all the best places in the home is of lesser importance to their survival than it is to wild animals. So, they have often moved away from the instinctive behaviours associated with it, using dominance and submission instead as general communication tools between individuals in specific situations.

With this in mind a dog can be fearful and submissive, but they can also be relaxed and submit to another dog. Every behaviour has an internal state related to it. Whether conflict occurs will depend on individual dogs, their natural dynamic and the willingness of one to defer to another amongst many other variables of any encounter.

When we live with a dog that has learned to default to reactive behaviour we rarely see pure, natural interactions between them and other dogs. We are usually on edge, along with our dogs and interactions are fraught and stressful all round. We can usually change that though, with skilled coaching that empowers the dog and raises their stress threshold whilst building their capacity for personal resilience.

Moderate to Severe Signs of Stress

When mild signs of stress are shown, the dog is likely to be still under threshold and able to cope. In fact he may not reach threshold at all if these signs are recognised and the environment is swiftly changed to meet his need and request for space. The more often these early signals are recognised and adhered to, the more faith a dog will have in his guardian to keep him safe and maintain the space that he needs.

However, if the initial signals go unnoticed, the dog will definitely experience an increasingly severe stress reaction and will move into his personal default coping strategy. Whilst we know that dogs experience fight, flight or freeze reactions they may also become hyper aroused and unmanageable. For the unenlightened observer this may be interpreted as naughtiness or dominance; however, a good dog guardian or professional will recognise it as the expression of a stressed internal state.

Increasing stress may trigger the following behaviours;

- Sitting or lying down, usually focussed on the stress trigger.
- The body tenses up and the facial muscles tense, ears are often pulled up and back as part of facial tension.
- The dog will lower their body and tuck the tail beneath them.
- Trying to turn away and creep away from the trigger.
- Escape the situation as quickly as possible, whilst also moving slowly as a natural instinct to prevent an attack.
- Paws may sweat and leave marks on the floor.
- The dog will breathe heavily, this may progress to heavy stress related panting.

- The dog may freeze, standing completely still and waiting for the threat to move away. This is often associated with learned helplessness – which describes the emotional shutdown of a dog who has learned that no matter what they do, they have no control over what happens to them, so they stop trying.
- Highly animated behaviour may occur, such as height seeking or grabbing at the guardian's hands or leash.
- Growling, lunging, barking and threats are a common repertoire of a dog that tries to chase the threat away. Often if the threat is not in the dog's safe space, this will be diluted but if the dog's safe space is invaded the threats will usually be highly animated.

Finally, any dog who has tried all of the aforementioned attempts for space, but has been ignored, may show aggression and even bite. Usually because they have exhausted their toolkit of less invasive attempts at communication, and see this as their final chance to stay safe.

An exception to the above is the dog that has learned helplessness, usually because they have tried it before and it hasn't worked. Ironically this dog is suffering greatly but to the unenlightened observer, looks like he is well-behaved and is far less of a problem than the lunging dog.

Individuality dictates that the signs used by a dog will vary. The lists above will give a basic overview of first mild signs of stress then moderate to severe signs. Try to spend as much time as you can, watching as many dogs as possible, and you will soon start to recognise even the subtlest of communications.

When you are greeting dogs, try to remember that eye contact from a stranger – within canine communication – is considered rude or even confrontational. Make a note of the mild signs of stress above, because they are also frequently used communication signals and you can use them to communicate your harmless intent to the dog. The use of these signals will show the dog that you are attempting to keep the meeting calm and risk free. Never approach a dog head on, but make your posture low, turn your face slightly away and allow them to approach you if they want to. This will give the dog valuable choices and encourage him to view you as a stress-free experience. Keep the knowledge that the dog will tell you how they feel about you, just by their own signs and communications.

Aggression

Dogs are not natural aggressors, they most often respond to a threat with aggression but only the odd few initiate it. Like any behaviour, aggression may occur for a number of different reasons. We must never rule out illness, genetic inheritance, fear, conditioning, medication and physiological changes as potential reasons for aggression. Each of these are possibilities and the individual dog will always tell us which drives their own behaviour if we watch carefully enough.

It is important to remember that a vast majority of behaviours we humans classify as aggressive are perfectly normal behaviours for dogs. They communicate with each other through displays and meta signals as a way to avoid fighting. Some signs of aggression can be very subtle and easily missed.

Dr. Kendal Shepherd explored the pathway to a dog bite in her studies on the Canine Ladder of Aggression. The Ladder of Aggression is a simple way to understand the dog's attempts at avoiding aggression before they resort to a bite.

The canine ladder of aggression is a systematic escalation of signs a dog shows when they are uncomfortable. As dogs are very social animals, many of the lower rungs are used on a daily basis, particularly when communicating with other dogs. This will maintain the peace and allow the dogs to express themselves and their current state of mind to others around them. Dogs attempt to use these same signals with humans as well, but often they are overlooked or misunderstood.

For most people, when they hear their dog growl, they think of it as a bad 'misbehaviour', and reprimand the dog strongly. Yet, the growl is just communication. If the dog is growling, it means all of the lower levels of communication have failed. Correcting the growl may make the dog stop doing it, but it will not make the dog feel any more comfortable around that situation. The growl is the last vocal warning before the dog snaps and bites.

Next time the dog is uncomfortable, he won't growl and get punished for it, but he still needs to make the uncomfortable thing go away, so he lunges and snaps.

An aggressive response often escalates through the following acts. It can usually be changed by changing the environment, but without the stress relief of environmental change, the dog will probably end up feeling the need to bite. The fundamental basis of the attempts shown below is a dog that is consistently asking for space. All the behaviours are intended to increase distance between the dog displaying them and the one they perceive as a direct threat to them or their resources.

Escalation of aggression:

- Freezing - where the body becomes still and tense. This is different to that of learned helplessness or the freeze that happens with fear. We often see this type of freeze when a dog is guarding something or as a prelude to a more exaggerated act.
- A low, throaty bark presented as a warning. This is a vocalisation of the dog's request for space.
- Lunging or charging but making no contact, a direct command to the second dog to increase distance.
- Mouthing, but with great control.
- Muzzle punching with the nose, this is often missed as a subtle request for space.

- Growling deep and low as a request for space. This is often displayed alongside a direct stare, by this point the aggressor is much more tense and closer to their bite threshold than the earlier steps.
- Showing teeth as a deterrent.
- Snarling, a deep growl with a strong display of the teeth, the dog is showing the only weapon he has by this point.
- Air snapping where the dog takes their snarl a step further but doesn't intend to bite.
- After air snapping has taken place and if the dog does not manage to secure the space that he is working hard to gain, he will move through his individual tendency to bite.

Whilst the above is a natural process we must consider the dog's individual learning, genetic influence and reason for aggression. In addition, the dog may or may not have learned bite threshold and/or bite inhibition. So, he might go straight to step four, five or even six in the process.

Aggression from an individual dog towards other dogs typically stems from one of two reasons. Either the dog was not successfully socialised around other dogs during their developmental stages, or they suffered a traumatic event; such as an attack from another dog. Some dogs may simply lack the confidence to be comfortable around loud boisterous dogs, but do fine with calmer quieter ones. Many smaller dogs may show aggression to big dogs but interact happily with dogs closer to their own size.

Distance Control

The reactive acts that we see in our dogs, which cause us the most heartache and trouble are highly exaggerated, yet totally natural, distance control behaviours. Distance controlling behaviour can be remarkably successful in dogs that have learned how to communicate with other dogs. Well-balanced dogs offer signals that ask for distance to be increased, or decreased, when communicating with other dogs.

Distance can be categorised into types and will always depend on the individual dog's ability to cope with the presence of others;

1. Flight distance is considered the closest point we can get to a dog before they run away. Most flight distances for domestic dogs match our own. Feral and fearful stray dogs have a bigger flight distance for humans, because they are less ready to trust people. Dogs that are scared of other dogs or people tend to have a big flight distance, despite their natural default defensive acts associated with the fight response.

2. Critical distance means the flight distance is overstepped and the dog may feel they need to attack. This is the point a dog goes over his threshold and becomes stressed.

3. Social distance is the dog's ability to feel comfortable around his peers. Social distance will determine whether two dogs are happy to share a sofa, with a metre space between them, or a bed where they literally squash into a much smaller space and many areas of their body touch. Social distance determines whether your dog likes to sit on your lap or your feet; or in the same room but a couple of metres away. We can breach the social distance of our dogs by constantly touching them or cuddling them, which will naturally put them on edge. After all no-one wants to be touched without inviting or expecting it.

Dogs will use signals towards another to increase or decrease the social distance in any situation. There are a number of distance increasing and decreasing acts that aid communication. If both dogs understand each other and neither offers a challenge, this communication type will usually be naturally successful.

Distance Increasing Signals

Distance increasing signals are often displayed as a result of the dog feeling overwhelmed in a situation. This may include play, or a simple greeting with an unknown dog. The entire aim of this type of signal is to tell the other dog to stop, back off or move further away.

Socially competent dogs will adhere to the requests. Dogs that are unable to read the subtle (or not so subtle) signals of other dogs will be less likely to follow the species rules of competent communication. Distance increasing signals are often shown by stressed dogs.

Distance increasing acts show a definite request to the other dog, to move or stay away. This type of signal will lead to conflict if the other dog does not respect and adhere to the signals which may include;

- Averting the eyes.
- Obvious head or body turns.
- Turning the back on the other animal.
- Moving away.
- Freezing.
- Head lowering.
- Raised hackles.
- Growling.
- Antagonistic Pucker.

A dog that becomes hard eyed, showing their teeth and probably also growling is displaying what we can consider an antagonistic pucker. As with many other dog signals, this must be read in context as it's shown for a lot of different reasons, including the intent of physical contact aggression.

A dog will certainly show the antagonistic pucker to ask for space, as it's a traditional distance increasing signal and, for most dogs, quite difficult to ignore. The antagonistic pucker is a display of teeth, usually delivered with a hard stare, to force the other dog – or even the human – to increase distance.

Other distance increasing signals can include common fear requests such as crouching and trying to look small, often accompanied by the dog refusing to look at the other dog, and showing a head turn whist averting their eyes. The dog that flattens his ears back may also be asking for space. A tense face and intended stare towards another dog is a sign of intention of a more severe action, usually not a good one, which is something to keep in mind if new dogs are meeting.

Our dogs, who default to reactive behaviour that try to send another dog away, via a process of showing loud reactions and threats, may move from an intense stare to a lunge. They could bark loudly and repeatedly, literally shouting at the other dog to leave them alone. All of these are intended to increase the distance by removing the threat from their immediate environment.

Distance decreasing acts are usually used by relaxed dogs, to instigate further contact. Dogs use distance decreasing signals to make friends, show they are peaceful and to tell others that they can approach without fear or threat.

Takeaway Points

- Communication is the foundation of positive change.
- Different dog breeds have different accents and to fully understand an individual dog we must first learn their neutral stance.
- Social skills are learned, every dog has a specific level of social competence which dictates how they communicate with others.
- We don't have to delve too deeply into their past to help a dog now. We can take a stance of moving forward from this point and help them cope, regardless of what they have inherited or learned in their life so far.
- Enlightened observation is the ability to observe a dog with a factually educated eye and understand how they are coping in their immediate environment.
- We can stop the escalation of stress by removing the dog from the trigger.
- Reactive behaviour is not the same as aggression. True aggression seeks to decrease distance and the whole aim of reactive behaviour is to increase distance between the dog and his trigger.
- The dog will always show us how they feel. We just have to learn what their communication and behaviour means and observe them with a critical and educated eye.

Chapter Four

"In order to really enjoy a dog, one doesn't merely try to train him to be semi human. The point of it is to open oneself to the possibility of becoming partly a dog." – Edward Hoagland

How Dogs Learn

Before we move on from the theory behind behaviour change we must explore how dogs learn. Whilst communication breaks down misunderstanding; understanding how your dog can learn to cope is the essence of building resilience and maintaining it in the long term. Whilst we can spend our lives acting like dog walking ninjas, attempting to protect our dogs from their triggers and walking whilst everyone else is in their beds, we won't empower our dogs to cope unless we teach them that they can. And we can only effectively teach our dogs, if we know how they learn.

There is a lot of jargon associated with learning theory. It can be difficult to grasp in the first instance, but it's really worth the effort because it will totally transform your relationship with your dog, along with how they cope with life.

Learning theory is the term given to what we know so far about the process of learning. It applies to all animals – including people – but in this case we are focusing on dogs.

Dogs learn in a number of ways and what they have learned will dictate how they behave. A straightforward example of this is the dog that has learned to fear other dogs, so their behaviour will change in the presence of other dogs. The specific change is also learned, so a dog's outwardly reactive and defensive behaviour, is learned by how it affects the environment.

Classical Conditioning

Anything that a dog learns is tried out in the first instance, then if the response to that experiment includes something the dog likes, the dog will try the same thing again – in an attempt to trigger the same response. If this happens naturally in the environment we can call it classical conditioning.

Ivan Pavlov is the name associated with classical conditioning, you may have heard of Pavlov's dog. The biologist learned that dogs can make an association between things in their environment and expect a certain consequence, without being formally taught anything at all. In Pavlov's

Dog's case – a group of dogs learned that their lab tech carers appearing in the lab preluded their bowls appearing, then the provision of their food. The dogs, motivated by the idea of food, soon began drooling at the sight of their lab tech caregivers – way before the food was touched. The dogs' responses in this case were involuntary, they had linked a few visual occurrences together and their bodies had created an involuntary response. In many ways like our own dogs teach themselves that when we get our walking boots out, they are highly likely to be going for a walk.

Operant Conditioning

Learning terms explain this further, in particular the things we consider 'the learning quadrants' which were presented by BF Skinner. The quadrants are part of a learning process we can call operant conditioning, or even training. They work by driving behaviour via consequences in four different ways.

Positive reinforcement means that the dog receives something they like as a response to their behaviour. Remember earlier when we said the dog must decide their own reward, it applies here too. The more a dog likes or enjoys the good thing that he receives, the stronger the displayed behaviour – that he associated with that rewarding consequence – will become. The word reinforcement means 'to make stronger' and in this case it's making the behaviour stronger by enabling or providing the dog with a rewarding consequence. For example, the dog sits for attention, so we give him a treat, and then the attention, providing double reinforcement.

The basis of effective learning is the building of confidence and empowerment of the learner. The dog that feels strong and confident is likely to learn quickly and effectively, because his brain chemistry is healthy, and he is happy. Dopamine is triggered – which cements memory, fuels motivation and makes the dog feel good. A dog that is getting things right in their lesson will be keen and willing to keep trying new things because his confidence is high, and the new things lead to a positive result.

Positive punishment is also the act of adding something to a situation that the dog sees as a result of his own behaviour. For example, a smack on the nose to a puppy for nipping. The idea behind positive punishment is that the dog doesn't like the addition so doesn't repeat the behaviour. Whilst it sounds simplistic, the process is fundamentally flawed. There are some good reasons to avoid using positive punishment as a learning tool.

When a dog gets things wrong his self-confidence will drop and he is likely to stop trying. Punishment is acknowledgement of getting things wrong, which also triggers stress because it often includes some trigger for fear or pain. When stress is triggered, the dog will experience the reaction we explored earlier – the reaction of fight, flight or freeze. Accompanied by losing trust in the teacher, confidence in himself and the ability to think straight in the situation this poor dog is unlikely to have clarity of mind to fully understand the situation, let alone learn something new. In addition to this, the ability to punish a dog at the exact second a behaviour occurs, so the dog can make the connection, is rare. So, the dog cannot see the reason for the teachers seemingly erratic threats or painful acts and becomes even more stressed and confused, so even less likely to learn.

Negative punishment is a little different as it removes something from the situation that the dog was enjoying. A simple example is the dog who is nipping hands during play, so the game ceases and interaction is withdrawn. This response seeks to lessen the behaviour based on the removal of something the dog is enjoying – which he should associate with his own actions and learn not to perform those actions again. Whilst negative punishment does not involve threats or pain – like positive punishment often does, the dog still experiences the confidence knock of getting it wrong, which may affect his self-belief and confidence to learn. How exactly negative punishment will affect a dog's confidence and wellbeing depends on their confidence to start with. Some dogs cope quite well whilst others would struggle and lose self-belief.

Negative reinforcement is the act of something bad stopping when the dog changes a behaviour that the teacher is trying to eradicate. Typical examples of negative reinforcement include a prong collar that is placed around the dog's neck and hurts until the dog stops pulling on the lead. The pain stops when the pulling stops, which is supposed to teach the dog to change their behaviour by relief.

Carried out to the split second and managed perfectly all of the above quadrants will work to teach a dog a new behaviour, or to eradicate an existing behaviour. Only positive reinforcement – and perhaps negative punishment in rare instances - considers more than behaviour change.

When we use positive reinforcement to teach something new, we are considering how the dog feels, their self-belief, their confidence, their brain chemistry and thus increasing their ability to learn. In addition, trust in the teacher is maintained and the dog is spared from as many bad experiences as possible. By its nature, positive reinforcement can do no harm to the dog. The dog can learn the wrong things if his teacher has less than perfect timing, but with practice this can be rectified, and the dog will stay confident and happy throughout.

Learning is happening all the time and is central to a dog's responses and behaviour. In some ways this can be unhelpful – for example if we accidently reinforce the dog that jumps up by offering him some attention. In other ways it can be really helpful, for example to teach our stressed dogs that their triggers are not that scary after all.

Life Lessons

Every exposure to a new factor in the dog's environment creates a learning experience. Seemingly random environmental learning is also called Single Event Learning. This accounts for fears and phobias amongst other things. What the dog learns depends on many parts of that single event.

Try to imagine the Universe aligning perfectly for one second. In this case the Universe is the dog's mindset, personality, life experiences, genetic inheritance, the exact split second we are in, the exact behaviour of the environmental factor along with anything else in the environment. Now, imagine taking a snapshot of all those things; and there you have captured a specific learning experience.

This 'snapshot learning' happens in a puppy's life from the moment they are born – accelerates throughout their puppyhood, adolescence and slows down in their adulthood but never really stops.

The biological aspect of this type of learning is what we call neuroplasticity, the ability of the brain structure to change. The puppy's brain when he is born is not fully developed. The puppy is pretty much helpless at birth and needs every physical need met, this is usually by his mother. As the brain develops, neural pathways are created. These are biological affirmations of learning. A neural pathway is the reason dogs learn habits, repeat acts and show fear towards their stress triggers. It's literally like a well-trodden pathway through the brain's neurons, that is established, so easier to follow.

At the very beginning, a puppy learns that his mother feeds him and a neural pathway is created that tells the puppy to head for his mother when he's hungry.

Later on, the puppy bites his mother's nipple when feeding, she responds with a kind reprimand and a neural pathway is formed. The puppy is learning that biting is not acceptable.

An eight week old puppy meets an adult dog and is attacked. The vulnerable puppy is terrified, and a neural pathway is formed. This puppy is at the most crucial time for learning and now his default response to adult dogs is fear. He won't need to be attacked again, to experience that fear because it's now the default route through his brain at the appearance of an older dog.

The same eight week old puppy instead meets a gentle, kind and playful older dog and learns to enjoy other dogs, from that initial experience. His natural default neural pathway is to see another dog and experience positive expectation of play.

The good news is that through neuroplasticity we can change the default patterns and pathways of our dogs. The nature of any route is determined by the first few steps and by careful behaviour modification we can help the dogs to choose a healthier route. They'll form a new and healthy neural pathway that makes their lives easier and removes their tendency to default to stress and fear-based reactivity.

There are two life lessons that occur when a dog is learning about the world around them and what happens within it. Every individual occurrence is considered a single event and that event is either worrying or normal.

If the event causes stress, for example it makes a loud noise or scares the dog in another way, it can lead to sensitisation. This means that the dog has become sensitised to the specific single event. A good example of sensitisation is the dog that is startled by a firework and becomes sensitised to bangs and loud noises.

Another dog may hear a firework and be so resilient that he soon gets used to the sound and it doesn't affect him at all. This dog has habituated to the loud noises as they don't worry or stress him at all.

The only difference between the two dogs described above is the snapshot of learning that we discussed earlier. Every factor in that snapshot will affect whether the dog becomes sensitised in the long term or quickly habituates to the sound.

Habituation may happen quickly, or it may take longer. If a dog is exposed to the sound many times in a short period, he may get used to the sound quite rapidly and then just get on with his day. If one firework is let of once a day for a week, it may take the dog a week to habituate. If we live with a dog that habituates to everything easily and rarely worries about any type of new experience, then we are extremely lucky because we share our lives with a highly resilient dog. However, you are probably reading this book because your dog is sensitised to one or more things, so their resilience needs to be built up and their sensitisation dealt with by building new and helpful neural pathways that empower them to cope with the world they are in.

One Trial Learning

One trial learning occurs when a dog is so startled by something that they experience immediate fear and the experience is so severe that the dog instantly believes they are in danger.

Just as dogs decide their own motivators, they also decide their own triggers for fear and this will dictate one-trial learning for them.

For example, a dog on a lead might suddenly be exposed to a motorbike that seems to come out of nowhere, the sound of the bike is deafening and before it passes, the bike seems to be coming straight for them. We know that the bike is just going passed but the dog lives in a world dictated by his own mind, and at that point could learn a fear of motorbikes – or even traffic – which has burned a strong neural pathway into his tender brain.

The next time the dog sees a motorbike he may decide earlier what he needs to do about it. He could experience the fear in the same way, but this time it defaults to the fight reaction – directly from his nervous system – because he's on a lead and can't get away. Cue reactive behaviour. The bike carries on passed the dog as it was always going to do, the dog sees the consequence and associates it with his own behaviour and the neural pathway becomes stronger, soon the dog is well-practiced at chasing away motorbikes and it all started with that initial snapshot of one trial learning, that occurred in one scary, inescapable moment.

Escape and Avoidance Learning

Anything that the dog dislikes may result in escape and/or avoidance learning.

Escape learning means that a dog experiences something they don't like and changes their own behaviour in response to the unpleasantness. If the unpleasant experience stops, the dog may associate that consequence with their own behaviour. Therefore, they'll try the same behaviour again next time. We see escape and avoidance learning in the use of devices and collars which result in an unpleasant experience for the dog.

An example which we hope doesn't continue to be used in dog training for much longer is the use of an electric collar. A dog may jump up and be zapped via a remote, the zapping could continue until the dog stops jumping up and the dog has learned to escape the electricity by stopping their behaviour. Avoidance learning is similar, but the zap occurs at the very moment a dog jumps up – in an attempt to teach the dog to avoid the electricity by not jumping up at all.

The above is an extreme example of this type of learning and uses the example of poor quality teaching methods, which will detrimentally affect the well-being of the dog. Escape and avoidance learning can equally apply to the dog that runs out of a house because the smoke alarm has been set off (escape) or refuses to go into the house (avoidance) because they believe the smoke alarm could go off at any time.

Chaining

The above example can be further explained by looking at a learning experience known as chaining. Just like Pavlov's dog learned that one environmental factor developed into something else and started to anticipate a consequence, the dog above may associate their guardian putting toast in the toaster with the smoke alarm so leave the house in an assumption of the next step – burned toast and painful ears.

Try to consider the links of a chain to fully understand this learning experience. A dog may learn that a laptop closing leads to walking boots, which lead to a coat, a harness, a leash and then their walk. So, if your dog jumps up at the sound of your laptop closing and you usually take them out shortly afterwards it's because he has learned your habits, beginning with learning a consequence and chaining back as far as your habits will take him.

Chaining is extremely relevant to the dog that shows reactive behaviour based in stress and fear. The links in the chain might lead up to something that is stressful for the dog, so their stressed behaviour begins earlier and earlier.

An example of this is the dog that reacts by barking and becoming hyper-aroused when you leave the house. We have a little Pomeranian cross who actually checks my husband's feet to see whether he's wearing shoes or not, then bases her assumption of his next move on his state of footwear. She will relax if her man is in his socks, but is on edge if he is wearing trainers. In her experience this is one of the first links in the chain of being separated from the person at the centre of her world. If we break the chain, she quickly learns the new links, she's an extremely intelligent little dog and a difficult one to fool.

Social Learning

Social learning is vital to the dog's ability to live in the world he has found himself in. Whilst other factors – decided at conception or via illness - may affect the behaviour of a dog, social learning is only achieved after a puppy is born.

The first social lesson comes from the dog's mother and in the case of carefully bred dogs, social learning is prioritised by the dog's breeder too. Interactions between puppies in a litter and contact with a kind and gentle human will contribute to the development of a confident and happy dog. As puppies grow, before they leave the litter, they will practice social skills and learn how to behave socially from each other, their mom and any other dogs in the home. When we meet a carefully bred and positively socialised and coached dog, they are generally naturally resilient, for they have had very little reason to feel insecure and any poor quality accidental experiences they have are usually overcome by their persistence and self-confidence.

A dog that doesn't experience birth and whelping from a secure and carefully managed environment will learn one - or many - unhelpful things that affect how they cope in the world. A puppy farmed dog, for example, may learn that people are scary and rough. Their mother may pass on her own fear and that first few weeks of the puppy's life are devoid of many positive experiences. This dog may be easily stressed, have little resilience and low self-confidence.

After the initial whelping period is over, the social learning for each of these puppies will depend on the situation they go into. Dogs always learn from other dogs in their environment and at puppyhood or even as an adult, the contact they have with their own species will dictate how they act.

Dogs learn by example from other dogs, in a process known as vicarious learning – which literally means 'if that dog does it, it must be what I should be doing too'. Therefore, if a young puppy joins a household with a well-balanced and resilient middle-aged dog, the puppy has the best opportunity to learn resilience and a sense of safety. It can work the other way too, if we bring an empowered and resilient middle-aged dog into a home with a younger and anxious puppy, the younger dog may take some confidence from the new addition. Dogs can learn resilience and anxiety from each other, dependent on the dogs and circumstances.

This process is all about the individuals and the dynamic shared between them. It cannot be pre-empted and if you are considering bringing an older, steadier dog into your home purely to settle a younger anxious dog be warned; the result of a new dog friendship can rarely be pre-determined, and you could just as easily end up with double trouble.

Vicarious learning is a wonderful thing to watch and can be used in coaching new behaviours. There have been a number of studies showing it in action, providing fascinating results.

Learning is affected by a number of things; motivation, internal state and the way that the lesson is delivered are all factors that affect learning.

The Stages of Learning

When anything at all is learned it ends up becoming a skill or a habit. This takes place in four stages. In the case of a dog who has learned to react to a scary trigger, the steps below show an example;

In stage one the dog acquires an ability to react differently to the trigger. This will take the form of coaching or behaviour modification which we discuss in more detail later on. It is in this stage that the dog learns something else can happen when they encounter the trigger and a good coach ensures that for this part – and the next stages – the dog stays under their stress threshold. Staying under threshold is made possible by maintaining a safe distance during the coaching process and only decreasing that distance when the dog is ready.

For example, a dog may be taught that the presence of a trigger at a safe distance leads to their coach delivering a tasty treat, so the act of looking to the coach for a treat is a new behaviour and the dog is learning that they really don't need to default to defensiveness when a trigger is spotted. After a while, when the dog is kept under threshold, they will feel safe enough to look to the coach for a treat whilst the trigger is far enough away.

Stage two occurs when the dog sees a trigger in the distance and instantly looks to their coach for a treat. This is a big step in learning because the dog is now aware that their trigger leads to something nice for them and a brand new neural pathway is being formed.

Stage three is the same reaction to a number of triggers in a number of different environments. The dog is generalising their response by looking for something rewarding from their coach, each time they see something that may begin their stress response. This is the stage where the new neural pathway is deepening and becoming stronger than the original response to a stress trigger.

Finally stage four of learning is maintenance of this new knowledge. The old, unhelpful neural pathway is no longer as effective as the new route through the brain. The new behaviour becomes the default behaviour and the dog automatically chooses the new response and will do so into the future.

Whilst this is a brief example of the four stages of learning for dogs that show reactive behaviour, all dogs are individuals. Some have ingrained fears and may never be completely happy or secure, they may always be fearful of their triggers and for their sake we must manage the environment for them. Most dogs however are able to respond positively to scientific behaviour modification, designed to build them up and empower them. Positive change is possible for every dog, it just might not be a complete change for all.

Learned Helplessness

Learned helplessness is one of the most distressing things to see in a dog. Common with dogs that come from puppy farms or that have been abused, this is a state of total shutdown based on a belief no matter how hard they try, the dog still feels unable to help themselves.

Discovered by Martin Seligman in an experiment carried out on dogs - with a view to understanding depression in people - learned helplessness is easy for a dog to learn and much more difficult to undo. The experiment included standing dogs in boxed areas with electricity conducting floor mats. The dogs were shocked through their pads a number of times with the inability to escape. After an initial flurry of activity and distress, the dogs adopted a depressed, shut down state. When the door to each box was finally opened, the dogs didn't believe in their ability to leave. This resulted in them being shocked again despite the fact that they could have walked out of the box and escaped the shock.

The dogs took much longer to learn that they were not helpless, probably because their initial learning experience was so severely stressful for them. The finer details of this study are brutal and extremely upsetting.

We see learned helplessness outside scientific studies too. A dog that has been taught with force, fear or pain may shut down in the same way as Seligman's dogs. Shock collars, punishment and intimidation can cause learned helplessness in pet dogs and if a trainer is poor quality, punishment and force based, it often does.

The lesson we take from it is that dogs will try as hard as they can to escape something awful, painful or terrifying. When nothing that they try works, they will believe they are completely helpless even when the opposite is obvious, and dogs need to be carefully and kindly rehabilitated if they suffer from this condition.

It can be done though, and dogs can most certainly learn that they are not helpless. They need the space to heal and the guidance to make successful choices. My own little dog has taken nearly two years not to flinch and to learn that she can initiate play and contact with people.

It's an extremely sad situation that a domesticated species suffers from learned helplessness at all. However, if you live with a dog that shows it and you have never experienced the condition before, you can take my word for it – these dogs can find their inner strength. With positive reinforcement, lots of gentle healing space and as much time as they need, they can exorcise their inherited demons and build their resilience.

Takeaway Points

- Dogs are learning from the moment they are born.
- Behaviour is repeated when it provides a consequence that the dog likes or finds beneficial.
- Classical conditioning is learning by association.
- Operant conditioning is learning by consequences.
- Punishment affects a dog's ability to learn and think effectively.
- Rewards and motivation via positive reinforcement enable and empower a dog to learn.
- A dog can learn to fear something by one single experience of it.
- A dog can suffer with learned helplessness and need rehabilitation to recover from it.
- A learning experience includes everything in the environment at the time the dog has the lesson. This can be remembered by considering the learning snapshot.
- The dog must pass through all four stages of learning to achieve full competence.
- Whilst some dogs will always be scared of some triggers, all dogs will benefit from heightened resilience and scientific behaviour modification/ coaching.

Chapter Five

"Some of our greatest historical and artistic treasures we place with curators in museums; others we take for walks." – Roger A. Caras

A Happy Relaxed Dog

This area of the book takes us into application of the theory that you have acquired so far. Every behaviour modification program must ensure the dog is mentally and physically prepared to cope with and learn the changes we wish to teach. Without preparation and gentle confidence building we are not checking and preparing the dog's general well-being for positive change.

The aim of the first step is to ensure the dog is in their best possible state of body and mind to learn new and helpful behaviours.

The health of a dog – in fact any sentient being including people – is split a number of ways. There are different types of health that are intertwined. Each of these will affect the others, as we have already considered when we looked at the physical effects of psychological stress.

When we are getting to know a dog, with a view to better understanding them, we can consider each area of health individually to build an accurate picture of the dog. To fully explore the dog's needs – therefore their overall well-being we are going to explore the Five Freedoms.

The Five Freedoms were initially introduced to outline five aspects of animal welfare under human control. They were developed in response to a 1965 UK Government report on livestock care and management, as a guideline of caring for farmed animals They are basic awareness of the needs of the sentient animal and were designed to enable the animal to stay in as good a state of health as possible.

Since they were introduced the guidelines have been adopted by many professional animal care organisations and are commonly used for pet care, alongside the use in general livestock farming. In this first step towards canine well-being, we will use the Five Freedoms as a guideline for preparing our dog for positive behaviour change.

Nutrition

Freedom from hunger or thirst by ready access to fresh water and a diet to maintain full health and vigour.

Freedom from hunger and thirst is simple enough to provide. We generally have access to fresh water and the dog food market is booming. Even if we don't buy dog food, a hungry dog will generally eat anything and like their ancestors they would happily live on our food scraps.

A diet to maintain full health and vigour is a little more complex.

The purpose of food is to supply nutrients to the body and brain, to support cellular health and regeneration. The process of digestion and the things that the dog digests will affect everything from their health and well-being to their behaviour.

Food is becoming increasingly linked to ill health though, for dogs and people. As we evolved together, sharing food was probably considered normal. We cooked the meat and the dog got the bones and scraps – along with any spare vegetables, peelings and similar food types. Up until a few generations ago our diet – and the diet of our dogs – was generally made up of whole foods with chemical free nutrients. Even fifty years ago, most gardens were used to grow food and many people kept the animals that they intended to eat.

Things have changed though and convenience foods, intensive animal farming and the use of chemicals and modifications has grown quickly over the last three or four generations. It's cheaper and easier to buy fresh produce in the supermarket. So many of us have stopped growing and opt for convenience. Lives are busier, working hours are increased and preparing a meal from whole foods is time consuming and unnecessary.

The result of this is that foods need to be preserved for as long as possible, because spoiled food eats into profits. Therefore, chemical treatments to preserve the life of the food on supermarket shelves are used often. In addition, much convenience food is far removed from the whole food that it once was. Processing kills nutrients and much of the convenience foods we buy today have been heavily processed. Whilst all this happens to the food we buy and eat, it does have one standard to meet, it has to be deemed fit for human consumption. There is plenty of legislation to explore on this, if you're interested.

Dog food however, doesn't have to be deemed fit for human consumption. The commercially created, canine convenience foods that we buy are not given the same health priority as foods developed for people. Yet the systems within our bodies function in the same way and both need a good level of quality nutrients to maintain full health and vigour.

Commercial dog food is being increasingly questioned. People want to know that their dog is getting the best food possible and we are starting to realise that the bright claims of health and energy on the front of the packaging, does not correspond with the ingredients on the back. With the questions come knowledge. It is this knowledge that we can utilise to begin the process of positive change for our dogs.

Whilst to be considered a 'complete dog food' by law, a food must contain all the vitamins that a dog needs in order to maintain a basic level of good health – the quality of the vitamin required is not part of the requirement. The food that this vitamin comes from – within the kibble or tin – is also considered largely irrelevant. And the process within which the vitamin is gathered, is not usually discussed either. When we really learn to read the ingredients in dog food, it's an eye opener and can be quite upsetting, particularly if we have trusted manufacturer claims that we are doing the best for our dog.

Dog food is made of a number of ingredients and each of them will appear on the packaging. The highest percentage of ingredient is written first then the ingredients list goes in the order of percentage, so any vitamins are usually the last on the list. The first ingredient of good commercial dog food will be a specific type of meat, not meal or the generic term meat, as meal simply means ground bones and the generic term 'meat' can cover a multitude of sins. The ingredients in dog food should be easily understandable, but often they are not. Long chemical names are used, in small type, outshone by the happy looking dog and promises on the rest of the packaging. If we feed commercial dog food, we should look for transparency and everyday quality real food ingredients.

There are two ways that diet can affect behaviour. It can affect the way a dog's body feels and it can affect the way the dog's brain functions. Either of these can affect behaviour.

Inflammation

One of the biggest factors in how diet affects the health of dogs (and people) is inflammation. A diet that the body is sensitive to, will lead directly to cell inflammation. Much diet sensitivity goes unnoticed. Inflammation isn't linked only to diet though, it is a totally natural, healthy immune response to irritants that are within or around the body. An acute inflammation is the body healing itself via an influx of stronger cells. Ridding it and any cells that it has damaged, of invasive bacteria or viral cells.

If an area of the body is cut, acute inflammation occurs around the cut site. The wound swells and heals, if the immune system is doing its job correctly. If a body is not cut, but still experiences a potential invader – for example kennel cough cells, the immune system will send an army of its own cells and this time the inflammation is contained within the body. When the potential for infection has been dealt with and the body is back to a healthy state, the immune system can withdraw its response.

If the body experiences a continued state of invasion the immune system will be constantly working to rid the body of the problem. This will lead to inflammation in the long term, known as chronic inflammation.

Chronic inflammation is an interesting topic and its effects are being studied in detail at the moment. Food sensitivities based on poor quality dog foods – or in fact any food or substance that is eaten, can cause chronic inflammation and if the dog is ingesting it regularly then the immune response is always working. By feeding our dogs food types that cause this immune response in their bodies, we can be subjecting them to a lifetime of chronic inflammation. The most frustrating thing is that we don't even know and instead think we are doing the best for our dogs. The reason being, that we have assumed that all dog food manufacturers create dog food with skill and intention for excellent health. A fact that we should be able to assume – but sadly can't.

Foods most often linked to inflammation include; sugar, saturated fats, trans fats, refined carbohydrates, omega 6 fatty acids, gluten and casein.

Commercial dog food often contains much more than food and if even one or two of the ingredients in a regularly fed meal, is perceived by the immune system as a threat, the dog will suffer with chronic inflammation. Which is one of the reasons we really must read and understand the ingredients of anything we feed to our dogs. In addition, if we feed kibble as the dog's only source of nutrition we are depriving them of the benefits of fresh food that would naturally support their immune systems and restore balance to the cells – allowing the immune response to dissipate.

So, with this in mind, what should we feed our dogs?

A diet of fresh food, packed with nutrients and vitamins and devoid of artificial colourings, additives and fillers is the ultimate aim. If we cannot provide that due to time restrictions we must choose commercial dog food carefully and fully explore the ingredients, then carry out external research on them. In addition, different food types should be added to the dog's meal – so they are not only getting dried food. These can include vegetables, fruits and meats, along with foods high in omega 3 such as oily fish.

All dog diets should contain carbohydrates, protein and fat through oils. Each of these three ingredients need to be high quality and if chosen carefully will also provide all the vitamins that a dog needs for good health.

Whilst I can provide an overview of what may be good and bad for the health of your dog, it's important to remember that diet sensitivities may vary between dogs, therefore some dogs cope really well with some foods and others don't. I suggest that you make your dog's diet a project. Spend some time collaborating exactly what you feed your dog and researching any studies that show the effects of those ingredients on canine health. If what you find in your research worries you, make some positive changes and you are likely to find that your dog's behaviour responds to those changes within as short a time as a few days.

How Food Affects Mood

The way that food affects how your dog feels is highly relevant to the dog who defaults to reactive behaviour when stressed or scared. Food dyes and chemical flavourings are linked to behaviour issues. A high influx of carbohydrates which are often used to bulk out dog food, can lead to an excess of energy that the dog needs to use somehow and thus leads to a change in behaviour.

Blood sugar is another factor that changes behaviour. A dog that does not have access to food for long periods may suffer with a crash in blood sugar before eating followed by a peak after eating. If the food is high carbohydrate, high energy as many foods are – to keep their manufacturing costs low - this will affect how the dog feels by providing a peak in blood sugar than a drop soon afterwards.

If you have ever not eaten for a long time, you have likely experienced the feeling known as being 'hangry' which peaks with low blood sugar and sends us running for the most calorific food we can find, to regulate not only our body but also our mind. The feeling of low blood sugar is a specific kind of stress and can be avoided in our dogs by regular feeding of foods that release energy slowly.

If we feed our dogs the right fuel, avoid problematic commercial food ingredients, feed them regularly to maintain their blood sugar and recognise their individual sensitivities, we will be soothing any inflammation that has already occurred. We will also be creating and maintaining a mood that best prepares them for building resilience.

Finally, remember that training treats count too. Many food types sold as training treats have extremely high chemical content and are far removed from food. Try to use whole food, single ingredient training treats if possible, such as finely chopped meats or something like fresh peas. Using chemically volatile dog treats for behaviour modification can be extremely counterproductive.

Comfort

Freedom from discomfort by providing an appropriate environment including shelter and a comfortable resting area.

Providing a suitable environment that enables the dog to rest physically and psychologically is vitally important. The first part of this freedom is simple enough, the dog must have a clean, sheltered and comfortable resting place that enables him to achieve a healthy and restful sleep.

Rest goes beyond physical needs though and a dog needs the ability to rest his mind and emotional state too, in a place where he feels secure enough to actually rest without the worry of being disturbed.

Can you imagine what it would feel like if you never knew if you were going to be touched, if you were woken from sleep by touch without warning, on a regular basis. You are likely to experience an adrenaline rush in the form of a traditional stress response and if it happened regularly enough you may even be unable to properly rest at all.

Any dog that is physically comfortable but never knows whether or when he is about to be disturbed or touched will probably be on edge. When we consider that a dog who defaults to reactive behaviour is on edge anyway, it's easy to see how regular and unsolicited touching can fuel that dog's stress response.

Patricia McConnell in 'The Other End of the Leash' explains our need to touch our dogs. She describes our evolution from apes - who are all hands. We touch to soothe, to show love, to make friends and generally do so as often as we can. Dogs however are not descended from apes and their communication does not involve this type of touch. Dogs communicate via subtle visual cues and unsolicited touch is not part of their communication repertoire. Dogs that are socially competent ask politely for interaction that involves touching and we really should respect that.

For a dog to fully relax he will need not only safe and comfortable physical space but psychological space too. He should be allowed to choose when he wants to interact and be touched, and be left alone and respected when he doesn't. Obviously sometimes it's unavoidable, for example for safety and health reasons, but generally in everyday life a dog will only be able to relax if he is given the physical and psychological comfortable space that he needs.

With regular relaxation and undisturbed rest, your dog will be more resilient and able to learn positive change.

Health

Freedom from pain, injury or disease by prevention or rapid diagnosis and treatment.

Physical and psychological illness is a fundamental reason for canine behaviour change, the following points are examples of this;

An older dog, who may have always been socially competent, might start showing defensive behaviour towards other dogs because of painful joints and the fear of being hurt.

A dog that suffers with a high level of stress may benefit from short-term medication which can only ever be prescribed by a qualified veterinarian (or veterinary behaviourist).

The dog may be suffering from thyroid disease which can lead to sudden onset aggression that seems unexplained.

A dog suffering with Canine Cognitive Dysfunction may need to be diagnosed and treated for the associated brain changes and possible depression that can occur with this condition.

The link between physiological changes and behaviour cannot be overstated. It is the reason that a veterinarian must be consulted when a behaviour change occurs quickly and/or severely. It is our responsibility to ensure that any dog in our care is treated for illness or pain.

Most veterinarians are excellent and will see the conditions that cause the dog distress – and therefore behaviour change, during a quick first examination. Conditions associated with ageing may include arthritis, Canine Cognitive Dysfunction and even dental decay. Vets see these things all the time so can diagnose quickly and provide treatment.

Other, less obvious conditions, for example brain disease, thyroid disease and heart disease will need further investigation and it's vital that a trusted and careful vet is chosen for the care of the dog.

The veterinarian is the only person that can diagnose illness and provide treatment for it. Whilst we must never deprive a dog of veterinary care, there are other things we can do to prevent the onset of lifestyle-based sickness. These include;

- Feeding excellent quality food.
- Maintaining a healthy weight.
- Keeping the teeth of our dogs clean and free from tartar.
- Using general supplements for joint care and overall health.
- Providing physical and mental exercise suitable to the individual dog.
- Avoiding over-treatment such as unnecessary parasite prevention treatments or annual boosters.

Vaccinations can often be replaced by titre testing – which means that the dog's blood is tested to check for immunity to certain infections. Most vaccinations maintain a state of immunity that lasts way beyond a year, titre testing checks the blood and the dog's body is spared the influx of extra chemicals which may affect their health.

Whilst a veterinarian must always be the first place a dog goes to if they are ill, or they show symptoms that may indicate pain, they are not wholly responsible for the health of our dogs. That job is predominantly ours as dog guardians, so the more we know about health and well-being plus signs that it has gone astray, the better.

The final two points in the five freedoms model are highly relevant to canine behaviour, particularly our responsibility to meet their psychological and social needs.

Expression of Natural Behaviours

Freedom to express (most) normal behaviour by providing sufficient space, proper facilities and company of the animal's own kind.

The fully domesticated dog is happiest with their human in their home. Generation after generation of evolution has determined this to be the case, so whilst street dogs and feral dogs live happily together in our peripheral, most domesticated dogs will live happily in a house, caravan, or even on the streets with their human. He just needs somewhere comfortable to rest, a supply of water, good quality food and respect of his personal space.

Like any other animal the dog needs choices and options. He needs to succeed at things to grow his confidence, to use his mind and body for self-empowerment and social contact with others in order to grow his capacity for social skills.

When I was a child, dogs were much more accepted for who they were, by the people closest to them. Over the last few years they have become an accessory for so many people and this has affected their natural opportunities to practice normal canine behaviour.

Some unpleasant dog training techniques have also robbed today's domestic dog of his natural rights. Behaviours inclusive of growling for space, barking, chewing things, showing a little tension over a resource or digging have now in many cases been labelled behaviour 'problems'. In the worst case scenario – through the least educated means – they are assumed to be challenges to the human in the home, thus lead to punishment which in turn causes suppression of the act by the dog.

Suppression of the dog's most natural communication and behaviour is unfair and can be dangerous.

In the scenario where the dog is expected to suppress or avoid using the natural behaviours mentioned above, the gentler natured dog may just go with the flow and live a life where their potential is lowered. They do this because they have learned to behave in a way that makes them convenient and easy to live with and have worked out that's expected of them.

The stressed, anxious, confused dog - or the dog with a strong character - will not adapt so well to forced suppression and may become stressed or eventually even defensive. This often occurs if the training approach is stronger, painful or threatening – forcing the dog to wait it out, and it's assumed the behaviour is changed. But when the bully leaves, the behaviour returns because nothing positive or useful has been achieved and the dog is more confused than ever. Or they may fight the attempt at suppression and end up either experiencing emotional shutdown or learned helplessness. This is obvious to the trained eye and quite heart-breaking.

If we find that normal behaviour is becoming problematic we must always look at what is triggering the normal behaviour. For example, if a child keeps touching the family dog and the dog is growling, the child needs to learn to respect the dog's space as opposed to trying to teach the dog not to growl. Touching a dog is not a welfare need for the child but having their body and space respected is a welfare need for the dog. If a child is not touching or looking at the dog and the dog approaches them to growl, behaviour management and modification is required. The child has an ethical and biological right to safety and the dog is choosing their own approach here. So, it works both ways and we must always consider the situation as a unique one, with unique individuals within it.

If a dog is a breed created to dig, and is digging the flowers up we need to acknowledge their genetic need and create their own digging space. If the dog chews shoes, we must acknowledge their biological right to chew and provide them with safe and tempting alternatives.

Social Skills

Social contact with his own species is a dog's natural right. One of the most common things we can be tempted to do with a dog that shows reactive behaviour, is avoid all other dogs.

We want to prevent the behaviour occurring, for the sake of our dog and our sanity – plus of course the dog that their reactive response may be aimed at.

Unfortunately, avoidance of other dogs as triggers will never help a dog to grow. If he is scared of other dogs, he will always be scared of other dogs unless he learns to be around them and calm at the same time. Most dogs that react will have a 'type' that they react to. This is directly linked to their fear or inability to read or understand that type. A small dog may react to bigger dogs with a defensive display but really enjoy the company of other dogs their size. A blanket avoidance of all dogs, when your dog likes some of them, may keep the peace but it won't help to grow your friend's resilience or social competence. Another risk of depriving social contact with suitable dog friends is that when an out of control dog does come your way, your own dog has a hugely damaging stress reaction; a response that could be avoided by achieving a higher level of resilience.

Now, this is vital, there are some dogs that can be a danger to other dogs and if you believe that your dog is truly aggressive please don't try to socialise him with other dogs without the help of a suitably qualified behaviourist.

Food Games

Other natural behaviours which have evolved with our dogs include their amazing sense of smell, their keenness to sniff out and find food. This innate behaviour uses both the dog's nose and mind - growing a sense of purpose. Just as we prepare meals for ourselves, we prepare a bowl of food for our dogs. Whilst this is great because being hungry can easily lead to poor mood, there are some more interesting ways we can feed our dogs. By using a dogs foraging instinct, we can grow his confidence and resilience.

Over the last few years we have seen a rise in the term 'canine enrichment' which literally means enriching the lives of our dogs by providing them with opportunity to use their natural behaviours.

The first of these natural acts is the ability to sniff and detect scent, which does wonders not only for mental health but also for confidence. Sniffing out his dinner in smaller bits will prolong that dinnertime experience and prevent boredom. It will leave the dog satisfied and able to rest after having worked for something he wants.

The second natural act triggered by turning some of the dog's meals into a task is problem solving. The opportunity to solve problems is an aspect of canine enrichment cannot be overstated. To find a task and overcome it, achieving a natural reward is promoting self-belief, confidence, industriousness and empowerment.

There are many excellent tips on canine enrichment available from many sources, changing problems regularly and allowing the dog to rip open a few boxes or collect his scattered meal from the garden is wonderfully empowering and promotes natural stress relief.

As part of step one of your dog's healing process it's a good idea to embrace his natural mental capacity, to help him relax then grow his self-belief. Remember though to only create problems that your dog will be able to solve on his own. If a problem is too difficult it will knock your dog's confidence and have the opposite effect.

Try wrapping food up in a towel for a sniffy dog or dropping it into a small box and half covering it with a cloth for a dog that needs a confidence boost. If your dog ever looks like he's going to give up before he gets the food then you have gone too far too soon, go back and make the food more accessible.

Chewing is another natural act that dogs will benefit from. Providing a dog with a natural, healthy and tasty chew is a great way to help him relax. As with all dog foods, take care not to use poor quality foods, rawhide is best avoided as it is extremely far removed from food and goes through a worrying production process. There are plenty of rawhide alternatives though, that are much healthier. Interactive toys inclusive of Kongs and activity balls will also use the dog's mind and inventiveness, whilst he works out how to get the food from the toy into his mouth.

Play

Play is a vital part of canine communication, relationship building and life enhancement for dogs. Some dogs never really learn how to play dog to dog, which is a sad side effect of being an only dog and having little social contact with other dogs. They may try to play, or even be desperate to play but their own body language is so conflicted with the body language of the other dog that they end up in a mess or even creating conflict. Dogs can learn to play with another dog at any time in their life. They may not be keen to learn as they head into their senior years, but young and middle-aged dogs may be open to the exciting new experience - even if they have never played with another dog in their life before. The first step of learning to play with other dogs is being relaxed around them, the second is finding the right playmate who is willing to teach, and the third step is an acknowledgement of mutual consent. Even if your dog is reactive to other dogs he may still love to play with one or two chosen playmates.

Playing with people is a learned behaviour, if a puppy is well bred and raised to play with people, they will respond well and be happy to play with humans for most of their life. Many dogs haven't learned to interact with people through play though - or have learned to play whilst the game is a bit dysfunctional. An example would be stealing precious or important items and running around or parading them, with the aim of being chased. We live with a dog that was rehomed from a family who couldn't cope with his stealing items then biting to keep them – amongst biting for other reasons. Vinny was an only dog for two years and despite being here for more than three times that, he still cannot play without wanting to parade and be chased. It's the lesson he learned much earlier in his life and meant that he got attention and had fun.

Teaching your dog resilience through play is a great way to empower him and to build your relationship. Like anything else, play can be learned through the right motivation and carefully structured short lessons within the realms of the dog's attention span and confidence. Games like tug of war pitched at exactly the point to let the dog win, will build his confidence.

To successfully play with your dog, in a way that builds his confidence and desire to play more is like any other form of coaching, except this time the dog is learning to relax and have fun. We begin by exploration of what the dog likes most, is confident to do and then we build on it in a way that he can cope with.

Toy play depends on how motivated by the toy, the dog is. A special toy that comes out during play sessions is a good idea and it can be used for search games too. Raising the interest in that toy takes some skilled movement on your part.

When I was a child, many years ago I used to play with the family cats by tying a bit of twisted newspaper into cotton and occasionally twitching it in the way that a small prey animal might move. The cats loved the game and I learned that if I waved the target 'toy' in their face, they ran away but if I dropped it on the floor 'lifeless' and it suddenly twitched, the cat's pupils enlarged, and I had their attention. Whilst cats and dogs are different, and cats generally are still active predators, the dog's ancestor once hunted too. So, this approach for many dogs will flick that switch in the same way.

Another example of creating confidence during play was used in my career training military protection and patrol dogs. When teaching dogs to bite the padded sleeve during their early police and military guard dog training, biting is usually new to them. The padded sleeve becomes their focus point in much the same way as my cats and their newspaper. The game was like a ping pong of interest. The sleeve was just out of reach and the wearer's body language small and discreet. Once the dog took the sleeve, he won it and the wearer let go, so the dog could win. Gradually the dog's motivation heightened along with their confidence.

When playing with your dog use your body language to encourage them. All dogs play differently, and some may need to learn impulse control whilst others need to learn that they can win something first.

Impulse control is taught by putting something the dog wants in front of them, teaching them to wait and giving a cue to take it. (A cue is a word that we attach to a choice, in the dog's mind, to show what we would like him to do). Then extending the time between putting the coveted item down and giving the 'take it' cue. You can then use it in all areas of the dog's life. For example, asking the dog to wait to have a lead clipped on. Or before releasing for an off-lead run, use a cue to wait then cue to release. The most important part of this is that you always cue within the dog's capacity, to ensure they get it right every time. Another important thing is that you assess first and if your dog isn't confident, have a few days of free for all play because if you teach impulse control to a dog that lacks confidence to play this could be counterproductive.

Watch your dog's body language and learn from him how he is reacting to your own. If he looks anxious, change your approach, if he shows signs of confusion such as sniffing the ground, scratching himself or trying to leave, then your approach is too much for him. Tone it down a little and think of the cat with their newspaper or the working dog needing to win his sleeve.

Some dogs become toy obsessive in which case this needs to be carefully monitored. A dog may play nicely with one toy but add a squeak to it and there's an obvious peak in their interest. This dog may grab and destroy, trying to 'kill' the toy. This can be counterproductive to building measured confidence, because genetic inheritance and obsession take over an impulse control drops. In this case, choose your play toys wisely and alternate with other rewards such as different food rewards or play through touch for suitable dogs.

Another thing to watch out for is using play to tire out the dog. Many people with high energy dogs use a ball launcher to encourage the dog to retrieve in a form of shuttle run. This is purely physical exercise and takes little brainwork for the dog. Like any animal – including humans – shuttle runs at high speed build fitness and the fitter the dog is the more energy he will have to use and therefore the more physical exercise he will need. This result of seemingly innocent play is disastrous to a busy, anxious mind. In addition, this specific exercise type is continually putting the dog in the mindset of chase, therefore a release of adrenaline occurs every time the ball is launched, a chemical that will fuel the anxiety of a stressed dog.

In addition, this specific exercise type is continually putting the dog in the mindset of chase. A state which - as part of their ancestors' ancient prey sequence -ordinarily would only happen for a few minutes at most in a hunt. The chase would always conclude with lots of relaxing, chewing and eating which can last for hours. When we continuously launch a ball, a release of adrenaline occurs, but the rest of the sequence - the bit that relaxes their mind and body with a sense of achievement and a prolonged meal - does not occur.

Finally, the twisting and turning of continued chase in this way can place unnecessary wear and tear on joints leading to early onset joint degeneration and pain in mid to later life. Chase has its place for many dogs, but for those with the potential to become obsessed it's better to try something else. For all dogs it should only be a small part of many other activities including mental stimulation and problem-solving tasks.

The key to play that empowers is enlightened observation - reading the behaviour and body language of your dog, then catering your own behaviour and body language to match his, making sure that he doesn't become overwhelmed. If the dog looks worried back off, to introduce challenges ensure you make them brief and easy enough for the dog to succeed – then let him succeed as often as possible. The benefits of this approach are canine resilience, self-belief and general empowerment.

Avoiding Distress

Freedom from fear and distress by ensuring conditions and treatment which avoid mental suffering.

This is a hugely important area of The Five Freedoms for those of us with easily stressed dogs. Fear and distress are more likely to happen to a naturally fearful dog, so we have our work cut out. During the process of initial de-stressing though, we can limit access to triggers as much as possible by changing the routine to allow the dog freedom from usual stressors.

At this point we can take some time to work out exactly when our dog begins to get stressed, then avoid that situation for a few days. We can even decide to walk at different times - perhaps even very early morning when everywhere is quiet - or not to walk at all. The activities we have discussed already in this chapter can easily be adapted to most dogs to use physical and mental energy without going out into the scary world for a few days.

Distress is part of life for everyone and though we cannot avoid it fully, we can work to avoid *unnecessary* stress for our dogs. Giving them chance to properly relax.

During the next few chapters we are going to discuss exactly how to provide your dog with a lifestyle that avoids as much unnecessary distress as possible. Alongside that, we are going to explore how to help your dog cope with the stressors that are unavoidable and inescapable, by growing his natural resilience.

Takeaway Points

- There are five specific freedoms that you can refer to, they will help you to ensure you are meeting your dog's needs.
- Diet will affect not only a dog's health but their well-being and behaviour.
- Commercial dog food may cause health and behaviour problems and it's vital we consider all ingredients of every food we offer to our dogs.
- Training treats can be highly coloured and packed with chemicals which make them counterproductive to training.
- Personal space is as important to dogs as it is to people. We should encourage our dogs into undisturbed relaxation and refrain from unsolicited touch when possible.
- Natural canine behaviour is sometimes labelled behaviour problems.
- Dogs need social contact with other dogs in most cases.
- Play is empowering, and most dogs can learn to play with people if they are coached with skill.
- We can never avoid all distress, but we can minimise distress and empower the dog to be able to cope by building resilience.

Chapter Six

"Fall in love with a dog, and in many ways you enter a new orbit, a universe that features not just new colours but new rituals, new rules, a new way of experiencing attachment."
– Caroline Knapp

Resilience

Resilience is a well-used term that encompasses many things but generally in dog terms means the ability to cope. Taken from the Latin term *resili* it means the ability to spring back from tension or testing conditions, with little damage. Physical resilience is seen in everything from the elastic band stretched to its limits then returning to its original shape, to the huge suspension bridge able to take the weight of many vehicles yet revert to its original form easily by design.

Emotional and psychological resilience for your dog is defined as the ability to remain flexible in emotional response or behaviour despite pressure from the environment, sometimes through long periods of time. Maintaining a good level of well-being and avoiding distress.

The basis of resilience is adaptivity. Therefore, positive socialisation is so important for puppies, because it builds their ability to adapt based on many different situations throughout their development process. A well socialised puppy that has learned about everything from loud noises to different types of people and animal will have a naturally learned resilience.

All dogs have resilience that they draw on every day. Environmental changes that the dog can cope with are examples of their resilience. For example, my rescue Yorkie will cope with being clipped by me in the home, but after being attacked in the park, she is less resilient outside the home and becomes scared very quickly. She's resilient in the place she feels safest and less when in a scary place. Her resilience is individual to her, and this is the same with all dogs (and people).

Another example is our most reactive dog, he's extremely sound sensitive and will bark at every trigger, in fact everything. However, he arrived with us after being picked up on the streets and is very easy to handle physically. He is resilient with touch – probably because he was handed around as a puppy – but he's not resilient around sounds.

Some have much more resilience than others and your own dog's behaviour will be undoubtedly based on his ability to cope, on his ability to stay strong and calm in his current environment.

A Metaphor

Imagine a small rowing boat on the side of a lake. There are rocks around the edge of the lake and the water is high. A storm comes and tosses the boat around but because the water is high, the boat doesn't hit the rocks and when the storm fades, the boat is intact.

Now imagine the water is low and the rocks are visible in many places on the surface of the lake – when the storm comes, the boat is likely to be bashed off the rocks and broken in many places.

If we assume that the water is resilience, the boat is our dog and the storm and rocks are his life's stressors, we can see how the resilience level will either help the dog through the storm - or allow for damage to the dog's emotional and psychological health.

If we rise the water level to as high as it can possibly be, the storm may not even toss the boat around at all. If we raise our dog's resilience to as high a level as it can possibly be, we empower them to live in this world which they currently cannot cope so well with.

Resilience has been studied for some time by psychologists and doctor considering human health and well-being. Whilst few studies have taken place on the resilience of dogs, we can still learn from studies on the topic and in many ways use them to better understand how to help the worried dog.

Just as we can understand an individual's behaviour through the process of careful observation and information gathering, we can also understand their resilience to an extent. To do this we need to consider the following three points.

- Trait Theory
- Protection
- Learned

Trait Theory

Trait theory assumes that an individual is naturally resilient as part of their overall nature. This specific theory is linked to genetic inheritance and how the chemistry in an individual brain works. In studies on serotonin - with people - it has been found that some people have a variant of the gene 5HTT and naturally produce more serotonin, thus are more able to stay calm and relaxed during stressful times.

Other people have been found to have a variant of the 2-adrenoreceptor gene, leading to excessive production of the adrenaline. Meaning that they may respond more to any stress trigger in the environment, than others.

In addition, whilst we know that people (and dogs) have a capacity for neuroplasticity within the brain, the exact capacity to form new neural pathways – for people – is also considered an individual trait based in part on genetic inheritance.

As with nature and nurture though, only some of an individual's behaviour has a genetic base. There are many other factors that make a personality. Or in this case specifically, the ability to cope.

Protection

Protection as a contributor to resilience – in people – is the receipt of parental warmth. When a child is fully parented with protection from stressors as they grow, they are thought to become naturally resilient as they reach adulthood. This is a baseline of growth in secure circumstances.

In canine terms protection can be considered excellent breeding, and excellent socialisation through the early growth and sensitive periods. Unfortunately, there's a lot of scope and capacity for that to go wrong. Everything from puppy farms to early isolation can lower the dog's resilience through deprivation of protection.

Learning

Learning resilience is the third possible point that makes up an individual's coping profile. Stressors and triggers are experienced then used to build and gain confidence until a higher level of resilience is created and the ability to cope is greatly improved.

Learning to cope in a way that builds greater resilience to stressors is not a case of throwing a dog into an environment though and overwhelming them until they cope. This is a process called flooding and which causes an acute stress response and in the long term a chronic stress response.

Nor is it a matter of pushing them into situations to teach them to bounce back. This approach would cause trigger stacking and probably long-term stress.

Improving a dog's natural resilience is about carefully managing exposure to their stressors, at a level they can cope, then gradually increase the stressors in proximity whilst naturally building the dog's ability to cope.

Resilience can also be fluid throughout the dog's life. For example, a dog that was once bold and strong earlier in his life may develop joint issues in later life. If he gets a knock by a dog he may start to show reactive responses to other dogs – these other dogs are linked in his mind with a painful experience.

Resilience and individual ability to cope is always present for a dog. The water level may rise and drop. At some points the water may be low when a storm comes, or the dog may be emotionally stronger when all is calm, but over time with practice and care, we can lift the height of the water by empowering our dogs.

PTSD

Sometimes things happen in life that are not part of ordinary day to day living and they are too severe for resilience to manage, leaving the individual bashed and bruised. Post-traumatic stress disorder is a condition that can arise from trauma such as being abused, attacked or physically hurt. Severe PTSD is usually experienced when an individual is triggered to fear for their life and leads to flashbacks of the incident which create the same emotional and psychological response.

As part of previously experiencing a crippling sense of danger - the dog who suffers a serious trauma is likely to suffer PTSD and become hypervigilant.

This is something we can relate to if we have seen one of our own dogs attacked. We start to avoid all other dogs when out walking our own and if a dog races up to us we experience an adrenaline burst.

Hypervigilance based on PTSD originates in the brain. The brain and nervous system's role are to keep the individual safe, therefore a heightened arousal state based on a real experience is maintained. The symptoms of hypervigilance in dogs include constant looking and listening for triggers in the environment and an inability to relax. The dog who suffers regular hyperarousal is closer to their own default fight, flight or freeze state. This is part of the reason we must teach and encourage relaxation and de-stressing activities before we start to introduce behaviour change skills.

Behaviour Strategy

Every dog will adopt default coping strategies linked with emotional response. There is no good or bad to a dog's coping strategy or even their behaviour, it's simply how they have learned to cope.

For example, one of my dogs fears large black dogs. Unfortunately, any gentle giant black Labrador instils fear into my terrier and whilst there may be a historical reason for this, I have never seen one. When Chips sees a big black dog in the distance he opens a little door in his mind and lets out a behavioural response to that fear. In his case it's hyperarousal and the stare of doom. If the distance to the passer by decreased it would likely be much more overt behaviour – but we always increase the distance until Chips feels secure enough to go about his walk. The behavioural response is then locked back behind the door and we all get on with our day.

All emotional responses have mind doors much like Chips' does, they are our neural pathways.

If a dog goes too close to three different environmental triggers he may have three different doors with their specific behavioural responses behind them. For example, his small dog friend that he walks with every day may trigger a *happy* emotional response, whilst the worrying Bernese Mountain dog with no visible eyes and confusing body language might trigger a tirade of defensive snarls and barks – because the *fear* door has been opened. Yet when he's tired and on the way home, your dog might pass a steady older dog that he is not worried by and feel *no strong emotion*, his behavioural response is just to pass calmly and take a treat when the other dog is at his closest.

Your dog's behaviour strategy in response to a strong emotion will depend on a few different things. It will be dictated randomly at first experience, the dog chooses there and then how to respond to the trigger. Then as the strategy is practiced, the dog finds it easier to default to that same strategy. An excellent reinforcer for any behaviour is the idea that it has worked to change something in the environment, to favour the dog.

For example, if a young dog is approached by a young child, arms waving. The child is unwelcome because they are acting oddly and frankly terrifying. The dog is suddenly very scared and makes a snap decision on how to react. He can hide or try to counter scare the *threat* away. So, the dog tries barking. The child stops and is quickly retrieved by a concerned parent and the dog feels safe again. Next time a young child comes his way, that dog will draw on his small bank of *scary child* memories and he is likely to bark a fraction sooner. Soon the barking becomes that dog's coping strategy and he may try it out on anything that makes him scared. With practice, he may begin using the same strategy on anything that makes him even slightly uneasy and within a few years we have a dog that barks at everything, just because it's how he has learned to cope with things that he doesn't know enough about.

Positive or Negative Bias

All animals alive today have an innate negative bias at some level. As part of evolution, negative bias has kept all successful species' alive long enough to reproduce and grow in numbers. If an animal sees danger where there is none, that animal is much more likely to stay alive than the animal that sees no danger when it's everywhere. Even when there is very little danger in the animal's life – or even the humans – the part of the brain which evolved to look for that danger is still there. This leads to all sorts of problems in the modern lifestyle and can play a big part in stress and fear of perceived threats.

Negative bias is an expectation of the worst possible outcome from an experience. In the case of dogs that react to triggers in the environment, their negative view has convinced the dog that the trigger is a danger to them, starting the stress reaction. A negative dog will default to stranger danger, as soon as someone new gets too close for comfort. Negative personality types will see danger everywhere, whereas positive outlook dogs won't.

The nature of positive bias is to expect the best outcome from a situation. Puppies are generally positive if they have been raised without a need to be fearful. A nurtured puppy will see a stranger and immediately see them as a friend. As he gets older and without learning otherwise, the puppy may tire of playing with every dog they meet and simply say hello to the new dog and move on. Despite their social interaction changing, the canine optimist will still expect the other dog to be friendly and greet without conflict.

Because the positive outlook dog is calm, particularly in comparison to the negative bias dog, he tends to have more head space to make measured and well considered choices about his own behaviour. Whereas the negative dog may see a trigger, immediately fly into survival mode and go directly over threshold – then react in just two or three seconds. One of the reasons we aim to build positive bias is to increase the available time for the dog's decision making process, providing them with the head space required to make healthy choices about their own behaviour.

You can learn through observing your own dog whether they expect positive or negative results from an environmental trigger or something they try. If they react with fight, flight or freeze to something in the distance they are expecting the worst from the thing they see and are being negative. If they are keen, happy and relaxed when they see a potential trigger, the dog is expecting the best from the meeting and being positive.

As you're reading this book and it is about building resilience in place of reactivity I suspect that you consider your dog has a negative bias by this point. All is not lost though because we can teach positive bias, as part of growing the confidence of our dogs and offering them the tools for empowerment.

In its most simple form, teaching your dog to expect positive results is showing him that most circumstances end with a successful result. We can do this in simple steps that work together to build a foundation, upon which we can grow your dog's confidence and resilience, in place of fear and reactivity.

Choice

The purpose of providing our dogs with choices is not only to give them as much freedom as possible in their domestic lives but it's also to empower them with the belief that they can choose to do something and succeed at it.

Dogs get few choices as to how they live and respond to things in their environment. For example, my dog who is walking along a forest track sees another dog that worries him. The other dog is approaching head on and the tension in my dog's body is growing. My dog's choice in this circumstance is completely dictated by my own, for example;

I can put him on the lead and keep walking him towards the other dog, giving him no option to avoid his trigger. This will **heighten his stress and my dog is likely to react, which is disempowering.**

I can put him on the lead and take him back, thus increasing the distance between my dog and his trigger but tethering him. **This will cause the stress levels to lower but is taking away his potential to make a choice, so it will disempower my dog.**

I could take him to the side of the path, distract him and give him treats until the trigger has passed. This approach will distract him and **allow him to make a choice** to take the treats - whilst also rewarding that choice in a response that will **empower my dog.** This is not wise to do if my own dog is close to threshold or the other dog is off lead and likely to invade my dog's space, it should only be carried out if the distance between my dog and his trigger is easy to maintain. If the dog is at risk of approaching us my dog is likely to react.

I could turn and walk quickly the other way, giving **my dog a choice to follow**, stay still or approach the dog. This is **empowering the dog** and providing the life reward of being able to leave a tense situation. Which is the basis of the teachings of Behaviour Adjustment Training from Grisha Stewart. Again, it's vital to do this within managed situations and with the ability to properly read your dog's reaction and intention. If the situation dictates for safety, a lead is always an option.

It's important to note, in the example above, that my own dog has an excellent recall. A dog that doesn't recall well should be taught that as a priority.

The final option that I could take here is management. Management is the fundamental basis of all choices that our dogs make. For example, if we want to change behaviour such as lunging and barking at other dogs - whilst on a walk we could choose to walk in a field where the space can be managed very differently. We can move around other dogs, avoiding the direct head-on approach and keeping my own dog's triggers at a safe distance.

The Unique Dog

Everything we have covered so far leads us to this point. The individuality of each dog is paramount in your investigation and approach to helping change his behaviour strategies and resilience.

Personality is as unique for your dog as it is for you, me and every dog that you ever work with or meet. Investigation of that personality is the basis of enlightened change, yet we don't need to spend too much time looking at the past. We can learn about the dog's personality by observing him now.

We view the human personality by how we see ourselves, others and the worlds around us. We can take a similar approach to each dog that we work with, including the ones we live with.

Whilst we can't change genetic inheritance, we can tweak all other areas of a dog's personality by working with their individual mixture of emotions, attachments, habits, experiences, expectations and responses. We can change their responses by managing their expectations and therefore their emotional experience.

The first thing we do is address the dog's responses and self-belief in the world. This can be done by recognising a tendency for negative bias and teaching the dog that the outcome of their behaviour or the presence of something in the environment, can lead to success, in as many ways as possible. This is the point we begin coaching the dog's positive outlook and growing their resilience by setting up situations where they learn that they can and stop practicing the idea that they can't.

Takeaway Points

- Resilience is the ability to cope and a dog that shows reactive behaviour usually has low resilience.
- Personality dictates resilience but it can be learned and taught.
- All dogs are unique in personality.
- All animals and humans have evolved with a negative bias to keep us safe.
- Dogs that are reactive to triggers are reacting to their own negative bias and expecting the worst.
- Fear can be learned in one scary experience.
- Phobias are an anxiety disorder and cause crippling fear for the sufferer.
- We can undo or lessen any fear or phobia that has been learned by empowering the dog and building resilience, then working with positive learning theory to change the dog's experience of the trigger.
- The first thing we must do is build the dog's self-belief, empower them and grow their resilience to triggers, this will naturally shift them from negative bias to an expectation of success.

Chapter Seven

"The old saw about old dogs and new tricks only applies to certain people."
– Daniel Pinkwater

Canine Coaching

We already know how dogs learn, so in this chapter we are going to explore applied learning through canine coaching.

We choose coaching because the role of a coach is not to teach something from outside the dog – coaching is aiding the dog to find and apply their own inner strengths and abilities. The canine coach will prompt and guide the dog but ultimately the dog is unlocking his innate abilities, those that have been damaged or lost in his life so far - thus enabling him and empowering him for the rest of his life.

It will help at this point to consider the dog's unique personality via observation and gathering information. If you are working with your own dog, or a client and their dog, it's a good idea to start a journal which will aid assessment and clarification along with logging progress which can get a bit lost on a bad day.

The first part of coaching with any dog is exploration. Asking questions and gathering information on your dog's individuality is key to successful coaching.

A Coaching Session

Even if you have never taught your dog anything, you can create a successful coaching session which will empower your dog and help him to expect a successful outcome. There are a few ingredients to a successful canine coaching session and they all need to be present, to achieve an all-round excellent result.

The Coach

Whether you are a professional that has worked with many dogs, or a new dog guardian with your first canine friend, it's imperative at this point to consider yourself a canine coach. Your role is to bring out the innate strength in the dog that you're working with.

For a long time, dog training has been all about the trainer. The trainer has been considered the partner with the skill and the dog is secondary. Thankfully though – due to a rise in empathy and awareness towards the domestic dog – many of us are taking a different approach.

As a canine coach you too are taking part in the dog training revolution. Together we are recognising that dogs are not so dissimilar to ourselves. We know that most of them were born with an innate resilience and openness to the world, and that their experiences along the way have pushed their strength deep down inside. We also know that we don't have to add something to the personality of our dogs, not strictly speaking, we just need to unlock that ability and strength and teach the dog to use it.

If all dogs were well bred and perfectly raised through socialisation periods, taught useful behaviour with kind methods and generally looked after – the domestic dog would be very lucky indeed. There are many things that can start the dog's inability to cope in the world and as we already know, when it's started, stress and fear can easily become habits that are hard to break.

An excellent strategy used by practitioners of Cognitive Behaviour Therapy is to start with the resources we have and learn how to move forward. This avoids the idea that we need to look backwards for long. If we are to utilise this excellent strategy with our dogs and add it to excellent coaching – we can move our dogs forward surprisingly quickly.

Ready Your Mind

As your dog's coach it's important to know that badly timed coaching or poor experiences during learning can be detrimental. Therefore, the first lesson is to only coach when you are mentally and emotionally ready.

During a coaching session your dog is learning from himself, whilst prompted by you. If you are feeling negative, unhappy, dissatisfied or frustrated, then your dogs' confidence will drop. In the situation where you're not feeling 100% positive, you can still help your dog by creating a food-reward problem for them to solve and sitting with him, encouraging where he needs it.

Set Yourself up for Success

Coaching isn't only about setting your dog up for success but it's also about setting yourself up to succeed as your dog's mentor. This can be done in a few ways, collectively grouped under the heading don't do too much too soon. If we expect too much from our dogs we are setting them up to get it wrong, or not to meet our expectations – therefore we are setting our own coaching experience up to fail too.

Keep it Short

Maybe one day your dog will be able to learn for twenty minutes at a time, but in early coaching that's way too long. Brain cells are interesting little guys. When we haven't used them to focus and learn something new for some time, too much focus all at once can cause neuron fatigue. Tired brain cells stop firing and the next day they may not fire enough to learn anything new at all because of mental fatigue.

In addition to current mental capacity, there is a point where a dog will learn something new and feel high and pleased, yet if we ask for the same thing one moment too long, the dog's confidence may drop. This may happen for one of two reasons:

1. He did it right and felt great - so if we ask again the dog may believe that he hadn't got it right and become confused.
2. He did it right and has learned something new, so repetition makes him lose interest.

Coaching is better carried out for thirty successful seconds than thirty draining and confused minutes.

As you learn to progress through your dog's growth in coaching sessions, you will undoubtedly at some point go beyond his capacity and interest. You will see a change in your dog's behaviour at this point. He may show some signs of confusion, disinterest or displacement behaviour such as sniffing the ground, getting an itch or trying to leave. At this point your dog is beginning to get uncomfortable because you are asking too much. You need to quickly do something easy and fun – then stop! Don't be too hard on yourself if this happens, we all do it and it's a great thing to learn from.

Keep it Fun

Play is escapism from reality and often has no aim but the game, it is totally voluntary and self-rewarding.

Coaching and play go hand in glove. As we already know, learning is facilitated by feeling good and play is relaxation and fun optimised. There's no reason why every coaching session can't predominantly be a game. Play is a vitally important part of relationships, it builds self-confidence and grows positive expectation. Playing is a mutual decision to interact – simply to have a good time and what better way to learn than when you're having fun.

The most important thing here is to adapt your play to the dog. Whilst one may find rough-housing and tug of war an excellent game another may be overwhelmed by such an approach. Mirroring your dog during play will ensure you stay at his level and don't overwhelm him within the game.

Be Prepared

Have your rewards and motivators ready to hand. If your dog likes toys, have them ready. If you're coaching with just food, ensure you have enough. There's nothing worse than seeing your dog achieve his best result and not being able to provide him with his favourite reward, to cement his learning and acknowledge his achievement.

A Suitable Environment

The coaching environment is one of the biggest aspects of a successful session. Teaching something new must always be carried out in a boring area. The less distractions there are, the more of your dog's attention will be on you. If you use a room in the house let him have a good sniff first. If you use your garden allow him to check out the area before you begin your session. Always give your dog the chance to toilet before coaching and avoid every possible distraction when teaching something brand new.

Later, we build distractions gradually for each new behaviour – but for now, the blander the coaching environment is the better your dog will learn and the more successful the session will be.

Motivation

Just as we need the promise of something to act a certain way, so too do our dogs. We are motivated by a pay rise, because we can afford a special trip, or we study dogs in general so we can understand and help our own dog cope in the world.

Motivation isn't just something nice that we use as a fine reward to look forward to, it's the fundamental basis of learning. To be motivated by something boosts associated feel-good hormones that aid memory and learning to be strong and fast. Triggering Dopamine is the aim when motivating for behaviour change, because this neurotransmitter is like learning rocket fuel for dogs.

Everyone's motivation is different and unique. Many dogs are motivated by food and even then, different foods have a different effect on motivation. Other dogs don't care much for food but really like to play. Enlightened observation will show you exactly what motivates your own dog, here's how to do it.

When a dog likes something, they will become excited and happy. Their entire demeanour will perk up and whilst from the outside they look pleased – there's also a lot going on inside – the most important thing is that they feel good and are perfectly placed for learning and behaviour change.

Motivation is used in a more sinister way by some trainers and this has a very different effect on the dog. Shock collars used for positive punishment and negative reinforcement are an example of this. The dog is motivated to make the pain stop so is forced into changing their behaviour, via escape or avoidance. Something is happening inside this dog too, it's a very different experience though. The stress hormone cortisol is released when a dog is scared. Cortisol leads to fight, flight or freeze and the dog is stressed so is as far away from learning as he can possibly be.

The dog that is coached with positive motivation will form new neural pathways and coping strategies. He will become empowered and competent, confident and resilient.

What motivates your dog?

Food

Food is an excellent reinforcer, because all dogs need it to live.

It really is a pleasure alongside being a necessity. Using food for motivation makes perfect sense and it speaks to the learning system of the dog, psychologically and biologically.

Problem Solving

There are a few ways you can use food to build your dog's confidence. To promote industrious thinking and get your dog expecting a positive outcome, you can create problems for him to solve in order to get access to food. To build ability, start with small problems that are easy to work through and grow the game to grow your dog's general self-confidence.

There are plenty of puzzle games and food dispensing toys to use for this purpose but there's also much that is virtually free. For example – for a low confidence dog, you could drop food in a low sided cardboard box. Next you could put a towel over the box, so your dog must get under it for the food. Then you could wrap the food in the towel and put that into the box and finally roll the towel with the food inside and place the upturned box on top of it. Each of these steps will build confidence for your dog and after a few sessions he will have learned to believe that he can solve the problem. He'll have formed a new neural pathway that, along with our work in other areas, will spill over into other areas of his life.

There are so many problems you can create, from general household tools and even waste materials such as old cardboard tubes, that will build your dog's tendency to become industrious. Remember to make every problem manageable for your dog's current confidence level, build the problem when they find it easy and introduce new problems that your dog will succeed at, on a regular basis.

We have an otherwise redundant room in our house with at least thirty problems to solve, we add to it all the time and our dogs spend thirty to forty minutes a day building their self-belief in there. They climb the furniture, rip cardboard boxes, wander into cupboards, sniff through shredded paper and work through their range of puzzles. The room is a real mess, but the dogs are very happy indeed.

Positive Reinforcement

Food reward is the real foundation of positive reinforcement. Whilst other types of positive reinforcement can be extremely powerful, food is a magical learning tool.

Use it cleverly though to get the best results. Food rewards need to be big enough to taste but small enough to leave the dog wanting more. The necessity for chewing should be avoided as it's distracting and breaks the dog's thought pattern.

Type of food should depend on the dog. If you have a particularly hungry dog, you may be able to motivate him with small treats, something as easy as frozen peas or blueberries. If you have a fussier dog - you may need to use something more tempting to trigger his interest and motivation to get involved.

Many of the smaller dogs bred for companionship are the most challenging coaching subjects, whereas the working dogs such as Labradors and German Shepherds are already part wired to work so often less food motivation is needed.

It's a good idea to start with the most basic food motivator that will work. This gives you room to move into food rewards that are more exciting, during the more challenging lessons. The list below will give you an idea of possible rewards, consider level one the least you may need to motivate your dog and level three your secret learning weapon.

Level One

Daily kibble.
Fruit or vegetables – berries, cooked beans or peas are easy to handle.

Level Two

Healthy and natural dog training treats (watch out for the chemicals)

Level Three

Cheese.
Liver cake.
Healthy slivers of meats.

There is an abundance of variations in the above list. It's a good idea to test a few and find one or two of each level. Your dog will tell you which he likes best – his favourites will make him happiest and his choice will be completely down to personal preference as the first step in his empowerment process.

Finding the type of food used for coaching is a skill you can grow. Each time a lesson is harder or when your dog is learning a new objective, you can change the reward. Be careful about using high value food early on though as your dog may soon start to ignore the others, as they are naturally less motivating. Skilled coaching uses the type of treat matched directly to how much motivation and effort is required. The general rule is – the newer or more difficult a lesson – the bigger boost is needed by the reward.

There is a process for success when using food rewards. With this process used carefully you can teach your dog every new behaviour that you would like to become his default in any given situation. The basis of teaching for success will follow the steps below;

Reward continuously and don't allow room for error. This part of the learning process is based on swift reward delivery whilst the dog is in the position or showing the behaviour that you are reinforcing. When you offer continuous reward at the beginning, aim to be like a slot machine, throwing out treats like coins, one after the other. For example, when teaching a dog to focus on you treats are delivered swiftly enough to prevent him looking away.

Next you draw out the time between rewards, this will confirm to your dog that he has it right and strengthen the behaviour. So, we start to stretch out the time between treats but not enough that the dog looks away.

Then you can begin to use variable reward types to strengthen the behaviour that you taught by using continuous reward. Variable reward can work one of two ways, you can vary the type of food reward, so your dog doesn't know whether he's going to get kibble or cheese, or you can vary the delivery of the food reward, so that it's intermittent. Whilst the dog is focussing we can change reward types, which boosts his interest and maintains his natural excitement and expectation. Soon you can ask the dog to focus, he will do every time with excitement - it in case this is the time that he gets the cheese.

The skilled dog coach will use continual reward to teach a new behaviour and then variable reward in perfecting it. As the learning becomes fixed by the continual reward then variable reward is introduced, to cement the behaviour. If you move to variable reward before the dog has fully learned the behaviour, then your dog will become confused, so you need to go back to continuous and re-teach from the start.

Prompting Behaviours

To reinforce a behaviour with food we must first see the behaviour. General reinforcement can occur when the dog performs a natural act, without prompt and the reinforcer immediately appears. For example the dog sits and we immediately reward that sit then add a cue to it - the word sit - repeating it for future use.

Coaching and learning can happen quickly and with great success when we prompt the behaviours that we would like. There are three ways we can prompt an act, they are generally used together for teaching something new – exactly how will depend on the dog, his confidence and what exactly he is learning at the time.

Capturing an act is marking the behaviour and rewarding the dog the moment the dog carries out the behaviour naturally. The trick with a capture is that we must mark the exact act, at exactly the time it occurs. This is often easier with a marker – which we will explore shortly. For example, with a sit, you wait until the dog sits of his own accord then mark and reward that behaviour.

Luring a dog is the least empowering of the three prompts, because it shows the dog exactly what we want. It's useful at the very beginning though and works perfectly with a capture response. To lure you might show the dog some food in your hand and guide them into a position as they follow the food.

Shaping is excellent for growing industriousness and confidence. Shaping a behaviour is the act of rewarding in approximations. If we want the dog to lie down with his chin on his front paws, we would first reward the sit position then reward the act of lying down and finally when the dog lies down and drops his head onto his front paws, we offer the final reward. We may even break the steps between the three mentioned here, depending on the confidence of the dog at the time.

Each of the above are perfect learning tools that can be mixed and matched between situations. They are all made easier by the use of a swift marker, to tell the dog exactly what he did right at the exact time he did it.

Markers

A marker is an excellent way of pinpointing exactly the act that got the dog his reward. Timing is extremely important when reinforcing an act, the marker bridges a gap between the act and the delivery of the food reward to the dog. A dog can be doing four or five things at the time we want to reinforce one act, so the marker leaves less room for misinterpretation.

One of the most popular markers for canine coaches is the clicker. The snap sound is accurate to the behaviour within a fraction of a second and the only way a click can reinforce the wrong behaviour is by the timing of the coach. The clicker is a neutral marker that should neither excite nor calm the dog. Your behaviour, body language and responses will influence how the click is received at any point but the click itself is a neutral sound that simply tells the dog that he was doing something which earned him a treat.

A specific word can be a marker too, in fact anything that can be linked with the delivery of food can be used to mark an action. The benefits of using your voice are that you can use tone to calm or excite, whilst delivering your marker word to the dog. This can come in handy as you start to use counter conditioning and desensitisation out in the world to help your dog to cope with his triggers.

For a marker to work you need to create an association in the dog's mind. The marker = food reward.

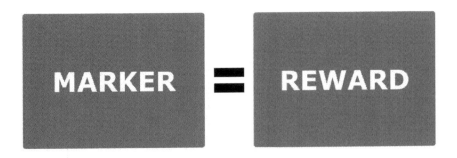

This can be done quickly and efficiency, simply by using the marker and delivering food simultaneously. Practice marker and food deliver a few times, over a few short sessions and your dog should quickly hear the sound or word and expect the food. Check that the connection is made by marking a random act and seeing if your dog looks at you for their food, if they don't – the connection isn't quite made, and more association practice is needed. When the dog has firmly established the connection, you should always deliver the food when you use the marker – otherwise the sound will lose its effectiveness and the marker won't work.

When the marker is learned and established, you can start to mark all the good choices that your dog makes. These can be the smallest choices to begin with but will soon grow into helpful and successful acts. Which we can gradually shape to replace reactivity or problematic acts which are currently distressing to you and your dog.

A perfect example of marking a good choice is the dog who sees something in the distance and instead of focusing on it, turns briefly back and checks in with his human. This is a natural act for a dog who is bonded with a handler or guardian but is so easily missed. In this case the dog has made an excellent choice when he notices a distant trigger, but if that choice goes unnoticed he will soon learn there's no point in making it and choose to do something else instead. Yet if the choice is marked and rewarded, by the sheer nature of positive reinforcement, the act will become stronger and the dog will make the same choice next time he sees something in the distance.

You can choose to work with one marker or a variety of suitable ones.

For example;

A calming marker may be more effective when you start work with your dog around his triggers where he would usually become aroused. So, you could use the word "calm" whilst holding a tough treat that may take a little work for him to chew. Or you could use the same marker and present a squeezy tube of pate or soft cheese for him to take a lick, whilst his trigger is in sight at a manageable distance (which we talk about in more detail soon). Using a calming marker in this way will not only reinforce the choice he's making not to react – it will also channel a calm response via a specific neural pathway, the dog is learning that calmness is rewarding.

You could choose a different marker for a different scenario. For example, if you're playing with your dog in a place where he is confident and happy - and aiming for a high level of excitement to teach him something new, you can use a heartily delivered "yes" with animation and lots of fun.

Cues

Cues are sometimes known as commands, but for the sake of dog friendly language, we prefer the former. A cue is a word that we can attach to a choice or and act – in the dog's mind, to show what we would like him to do.

When we put a choice on cue we set the dog up to succeed – but only when we have taught him exactly what the cue means. We often see people throwing cues around their dogs like confetti and the dog has no idea what's expected of them. Or the dog may have an inkling, but the cue hasn't been taught properly via positive reinforcement, so the dog is neither motivated nor capable of successfully responding.

A good cue is a one syllable word that is different from general everyday words. It is taught alongside the choice and reinforced carefully from the earliest instance.

First introduced during the choice/marker and reward process.

Then the cue is delivered before the marker.

Then gradually brought forward so it comes before the choice.

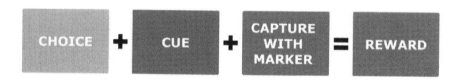

When a cue is fully associated in the dog's mind with their choice – they will hear the cue and know exactly which choice will bring them their reward and the behaviour will be learned.

This knowledge will help the dog to make the more rewarding choices and give him the confidence to succeed in more areas of his life.

Cues are not limited to coaching, dogs teach themselves cues all the time. If you live with a particularly astute dog that is motivated by something specific – for example the word "walk"- you probably have to whisper it because the moment it's uttered your dog is running circles in anticipation.

Takeaway Points

- Canine coaching is an approach that empowers the dog.
- All dogs have an innate strength to cope in the world.
- When a dog can't cope, we can help him to find the strength that he has lost along the way.
- Dogs learn best when motivated and happy.
- Food is an excellent motivator.
- We can learn to use food skilfully to optimise learning via positive reinforcement.
- We can lure, shape and capture acts we want the dog to repeat by using a marker.
- Markers help canine coaching because they help the dog understand which choices we would like him to repeat.
- We can add cues to choices – to help our dogs make the right ones.
- You can use multiple markers for good choices or stick to one for everything.
- We need to be completely prepared emotional, psychologically and physically before we begin a canine coaching session.
- All new acts should be taught in the blandest environment possible.
- Learning based in play is highly successful.

Chapter Eight

"A dog desires affection more than its dinner. Well – almost."
– Charlotte Gray

Practical Tasking

The practical tasking that we are about to cover is not typical dog training of cues and behaviours. We focus on things that will aid natural calmness for your dog, grow their resilience and generally enhance their state of mind via specific tasks.

The aim of this chapter is to use practical tasks to grow the confidence and ability of your dog through positive reinforcement. As with any attempt to change long term habits and coping strategies, we will start small and build the foundations for change from the ground up. Try to consider this area one of layered growth for the dog.

If a dog has been following one neural pathway for many repetitions, that route will be the default choice. Whilst we are teaching even the smallest new choice, we are forming and strengthening neural pathways that may not have been used for a while, perhaps since the dog had a scary experience in that type of situation. Our role is to make the new and healthier pathway, the easiest to choose initially and the default one in the future.

We begin by establishing a bottom layer of resilience and self-belief by empowering the dog via introducing and increasing new successes. We then build another layer on top of the first one, by adding to their successes and teaching more advanced choices. We continue this for as long as necessary with the aim of growing the dog's confidence. At the beginning the achievements may seem small but practiced and developed they will begin to grow and will improve all areas of the dog's life – changing their behaviour as a happy side-effect.

The methods we are going to use here are based on a relatively new style of teaching, creating managed choices and setting the dog up to take the right one. Choices are not only empowering for any individual, they are also an excellent learning tool.

We all make a multitude of choices every day. Some are conscious, and some are unconscious. For example, I woke up very early this morning because the dogs were ready to go out. I momentarily got back into bed but then got thinking about the choices I had. The first was to go back to sleep, the second was to get the coffee machine on, go up to the office and write this chapter. There were many other options, like reading a novel, checking Facebook or working on our education business. I then considered what would happen at the end of each choice and a new chapter was the most rewarding result, therefore the most motivating so here we are.

My choice this morning was made much easier by the fact that I have made the same choice most days for the last few weeks, early coffee and early keyboard has become a habit. Had I been choosing to fall back to sleep over the last few weeks, we probably wouldn't be here at all.

A similar thing happens within learning by choice for our dogs, but the process is much quicker and takes far less consideration. There are just as many choices that the dog can take though and without a doubt, the dog will always take the one which they believe will bring the best result. The habit will apply here too, if a choice is well-practiced, it will usually be the easiest one for a dog to take.

Our job as coaches is to make the healthiest and most helpful choice, the easiest for our dogs. For the best result we do that with play and reward. The reward is the dog's motivation and the games make the whole choice feel brilliant.

Introvert or Extrovert

Like people, dogs all have their own level of comfortable interaction and their own preferred social space.

Introverted dogs will be less likely to ask you to interact, they won't be keen on physical attention unless it's on their terms. It's just their nature to enjoy social and often physical space. Signs that you are dealing with an introvert are shyness, timidity, unwillingness to meet strangers – dogs or people, the tendency to become withdrawn and sensitivity to rebuff from those they love. An introverted dog is not the slightest bit interested in being cuddled unless they ask for it, constant uninvited physical touch is the introvert's nightmare, being touched at all by strangers is similarly distressing for this dog.

Extrovert dogs are less shy in the world and are outgoing, sociable and can be overenthusiastic and unrestrained on greeting. Extrovert dogs are usually friendly, unless they have learned that others are a threat – in which case they will likely be the loudest when trying to tell others to go away. With their human family, the extrovert will be consistent and enthusiastic. The well-balanced extrovert thoroughly enjoys meeting new people and dogs, but even they don't relish unsolicited physical touch.

Whilst some dogs are one or the other, most are on a sliding scale between the two. Some dogs are quite outgoing with people they know well but disinterested in strangers, whilst others love everyone. We can add learning and prior experiences to their personality traits and still get an idea of whether a dog is predominantly an introvert or extrovert by nature. Their nature will affect their ability to learn and their responses in both coaching and the choices they take on a daily basis.

Learning Style

The way that dogs learn - and act whilst they are learning - will vary. Their activity levels when learning something new really depends on their personality and individuality. Learning style also depends on the dog's confidence.

If a dog is unsure about his capability or the lesson, he will seem to lose interest. He may move away or show displacement acts like scratching himself or sniffing the ground. This is his way of trying to change the subject because this one makes him uncomfortable. This is the point where we must change the approach and quickly – because this is where the dog is starting to lose confidence, because he just doesn't understand.

The following descriptions are learning styles that you may see from any individual dog when learning to make the choice that we want to reward in a coaching session:

The methodical learner needs time to think, the dog will need space and pause whilst he remembers or works out the task you have set him. An example of this is my Yorkiepom who learns very quickly but is not a frustrated learner. She will stop for a moment and think, then rush off and do whatever she thinks is the right choice for her reward. She's a total delight to teach.

Methodical learners can also have low confidence and need encouragement. Waiting for too long without the dog getting it right, in this scenario will disempower the dog. Building persistence and industriousness via enrichment tasks is great for this type of dog. Problem solving is empowering. If you think you have a dog that is methodical but lacks confidence, you can encourage them by teaching lots of quick movements on basic cues.

For example, teaching a nose to hand touch on cue then moving quickly around in the space and offering the hand whilst giving the cue, most dogs love to chase and touch on cue. We will teach the hand touch shortly.

Carefully observe everything the dog does, offer an encouraging word or interim reward to give them the boost they need whilst not overdoing it enough to distract or disempower him.

A dog that's fast and keen experiencing the same lesson may go through a repertoire of learned acts – because they have been reinforced in the past. One of my Jack Russell terriers is a frustrated learner. He loves to learn but if his reactions ever get quicker than mine he's raking with his front paws and generally frustrated. This type of learner can be settled by adding a lot of calm positions into the coaching and teaching them patience, for their reward. The trick with this type of learner is to speed up your own reactions and slow down theirs to bring your teaching speed in line with their learning speed as a general average between the two.

Teaching Calm

Teaching a dog to settle or be calm is important for any dog who becomes over-aroused quickly or spends a lot of time in a hypervigilant state. Before we teach relaxed behaviour, we must be sure that the dog's needs are met, which we have covered previously. Meeting the dog's needs emotionally, socially and physically is the primer for relaxation. It's important that we don't fall short of meeting the needs of our dogs and in the same way that we don't overdo it.

An example of overdoing it would be walking a dog for many miles and growing his fitness to athlete level and wondering why he has so much energy. Walking in areas that lead to high arousal can undo any calmness that the dog has achieved. Or responding to a dog's requests to interact or play at every point they ask, when they ask every hour or so.

Don't get me wrong, in my opinion dogs that ask to play occasionally should be played with. They are after all entitled to choices in their life and if they have the choice to play – it's little different to us asking to play with them. If we respond with delight, then that empowers our friend and leads to an excellent, fun bonding ritual. However, if the dog becomes obsessive and requests interaction every time you move, or if they have been settled for just a little while then it could be becoming an obsession and is the opposite of relaxation. It's usually the dogs that are quick learners and easily frustrated who find it most difficult to relax. These are the ones that drop a ball on your foot in hope that you will throw it.

Remember that dogs are individuals, some are bred with a long day's work in mind and they need to at least be busy meeting their genetic needs for some of the day. Others are bred to be companions and they will happily stick by their people, with less brain and body work needed.

If a low confidence dog asks you to interact, that's an amazing achievement for them and worth celebrating. If a scared dog asks to interact, that's wonderful. It's a great opportunity to build trust and a mutually beneficial relationship via the ritual of play.

Teaching relaxation is a good thing. Dogs need to relax regularly, dogs that react to triggers are more in need of regular relaxation than most. Relaxation can be anything from snoozing for a few hours after a walk to spending an hour chewing something healthy and suitable and being really engaged in the activity. The opposite is watching and waiting for something to happen or listening for sounds.

When a dog is susceptible to stress on walks, he is likely to be trigger stacking throughout. Even if he doesn't react on that walk, his triggers (his arousal level) may have been raised a few times and he may return home more aroused than he was when he woke up that morning. In some cases, stress levels can rise every day when the dog is walked, then without stress relief exercises, the dog spends the rest of the day recovering.

For dogs that are having long walks and not coping well with them, it may be worth changing their schedule and making their life calmer. It's important we acknowledge that solely using physical exercise for tiring a dog out will grow the dog's fitness and yet still not use their mental energy. It can be easy to fall into the trap of providing longer walks and wondering why the dog is not tired. If that same dog gets stressed on walks, we are exacerbating their anxiety and exposing them to potential triggers for longer too.

If this is the situation for your dog, or any dog that you work with, it's a good idea to look at the current exercise schedule. It's a lesson in re-appropriation of time. Instead of one 60 minute walk a day, we could offer the dog a 30 minute walk and 30 minutes of something else directly after the walk.

This approach serves a few purposes:

- It keeps the dog in the world that scares him, for a shorter time.
- It gives less opportunity for trigger stacking.
- The dog still gets a good amount of physical exercise.

- Now the dog also gets a good amount of mental exercise too.

If we use what was once the second part of the dog's walk to either teach him calm behaviours for his meal or to allow him to search or problem solve to get his food, we are helping his readiness to rest. He's not only going to be physically satisfied but mentally too. In this case we give the dog the best possible chance of lowering their arousal levels and returning to their basal state of well-being.

This approach will set him up to learn that a quiet hour or two afterwards is part of his daily schedule and he will be likely to nap it away. When the dog's needs are properly met, that's the time to expect them to settle. This re-schedule is particularly good for dogs that constantly want attention and can't seem to rest. Attention seeking behaviours are understandable if a dog is not getting his needs met.

Attention Seeking Behaviour

Attention seeking behaviour may occur for a few different reasons. As with every other behaviour type, it's important that you recognise the reasons for it, before you try to change it.

It's vital to check that their lifestyle meets their needs, by looking at their breed, original artificial selection and how much mental and physical stimulation they get. A bored dog that is snubbed when trying to interact may turn his attention on himself and begin self-harming or displaying stereotypical acts like shadow or tail chasing.

If the dog is having the opportunity to use up his physical and mental energy though, and he's still attention seeking – it may be habitual and inadvertently taught via reinforcement. In this case it's acceptable to ignore the attention seeking and it will go away via a process of extinction (stopping due to lack of reinforcement) but watch out for:

The extinction burst where the behaviour gets briefly worse before it gets better. If this happens it can be easy to give in; but that's not advisable as your attempt at extinction has now become a variable reward (the reward that we use to strengthen behaviour)

Spontaneous recovery where the behaviour became extinct but has been momentarily reinforced in the dog's mind so comes back stronger than it ever was before.

Teaching a dog to be calm will include the following:

- Managed mental exercise where we provide problems for the dog to solve, to use his mental exercise and aid relaxed thinking.
- Coaching for calmness to teach gentle and relaxed behaviour on cur, to promote the energy of relaxation.
- Managed physical exercise where we ensure that we avoid as many triggers as possible by how and where

we walk the dog. This is something we develop into positive desensitisation a little later but first we ensure the dog is as calm as possible on a regular basis.

Impulse Control

Impulse control is a choice to wait before reacting. It's a momentary consideration before launching or grabbing and many dogs that lack impulse control can be difficult to handle, yappy or over aroused.

Arousal is the level of excitement or stress that a dog reaches before he reacts. It's his level of stress and depends on the ability that he has to cope, before he reaches threshold and reacts. We discussed this earlier when we explored trigger stacking. A dog that can't cope with much before he reacts will be more aroused earlier than other dogs, and he cannot stop and think before going over threshold.

Teaching impulse control will help that dog take a little time when he experiences a trigger. It presents him with another option other than going straight to his current default. This is a base layer of mind space, that will flow into other areas of the dog's life – giving him crucial new seconds to make the right choices at all new opportunities.

The following activity is an excellent way to teach impulse control.

Pause and Treat

Pause and treat teaches the dog two new and important choices:

1. That he has mind space to make any decision and can choose to pause before reacting.
2. That he can choose to check in with his coach and this is the most rewarding choice he can make.

Have your dog in a quiet, familiar area and take some small treats and your marker (either your clicker or a word). Wait for your dog to settle into a sitting or lying down position, as he will naturally be less aroused in a relaxed position. Sit on a chair if the dog is inclined to jump on you – or you can sit on the floor if he isn't.

1. Pop a treat on the ground between you, easily within your reach so the dog cannot grab it and provide his own reward. If you're sitting on a chair, you can pop the treat on your knee.
2. Wait.
3. If the dog makes a choice to try and take the treat, pop your hand over it to prevent access – when the dog moves away from the treat, remove your hand too. You may need to do this a few times in the beginning.
4. Soon the dog will realise that attempting to take the treat is not rewarding at all. At this point he will give pause, even though your hand is not over the treat.

Mark this behaviour and reward immediately by passing the dog the treat from the ground.

5. Repeat step five but alternate randomly between passing the treat from the ground or a new treat from your hand, whilst leaving the original one in place.

6. Repeat this activity three to five times and end the session with lots of praise and a favoured reward, a game is a good choice as play has recently been found to cement learning at the end of a coaching session.

After practicing pause and treat a few times you can begin to change the fifth step of the process, by releasing the dog verbally to take the treat. Giving permission to take the treat on some occasions is teaching something extremely important – to look for you for direction when he would usually do something else altogether.

This lesson around something the dog wants can be practiced in many scenarios, including when you pop their food bowl down or give them a chew treat to keep. Remember though to build distractions gradually and always set the dog up for success by being fully focussed – mentally and physically with every practice.

When your dog is making the right choices around food you can add the opportunity to make them in other areas too. If your dog likes toys, repeat the steps above with their favourite toys. Get creative with it and consider how many ways you can set your dog up to pause, before making the easiest choice which also suits a positive behaviour change. Remember that success builds self-belief and this leads directly to resilience.

After a few days, or maybe a little longer depending on how quickly your dog gets the idea, and by the time the dog is giving pause at every practice, he should be meeting your eyes when you present something her wants. He will do this because he's looking for direction from you and his choices have been shaped this way. This is the perfect time to mark and add a cue to the act of checking in with you.

This small segment of mental space is an amazing achievement for the dog who has previously believed that he needs to react before he thinks, to stay safe and scare the worrying thing away.

Another area of impulse control is perimeter learning which simply means that your dog learns to go to a designated area, within a perimeter and settle there until released. To be fair to the dog it's nice to make the area their bed or comfy safe spot, so they can settle comfortably.

This type of lesson increases impulse control and needs to be built in the same way, by making the task short and easy, then building the time via shaping.

You can teach the dog to wait within his comfy space with the following steps:

1. Establish the place you would like to be the dog's space. This can be a bed, open crate or a blanket anywhere at all.

2. Establish the perimeter. This can be the edge of a reasonably sized blanket or mat or the gateway to a nook of space such as the crate.

3. Pop a treat in the area, so the dog must go into the area to get the treat.

4. Mark the dog's position in the area and deliver a second treat, the one associated with the marker.

5. Throw a third treat away from the area so the dog leaves the space to fetch it, introduce a cue for leaving the perimeter early here because it will help you to establish it later.

6. Repeat steps three to five and add the cue for going within the perimeter.

7. Continue with the cue and drop off the use of a treat to tempt the dog into the area. You can do this first by pretending to put a treat down, then stopping the first treat altogether.

The above steps will need to be carried out over a few ten-minute sessions. When your dog is going in and out of the designated area confidently you can start to work on their impulse to leave the area. This will be carried out in the same way as traditional impulse control. By shaping, via a process of increasing the time between entering and leaving the designated perimeter area.

Perimeter learning is great for giving your dog a chew or stuffed toy, after the dog has learned his space, he can go into it and relax until you're ready to do something with him.

This type of learning is never to be used for punishment. The aim is that the dog learns relaxation in a comfy spot, as a form of controlling the impulse to leave that spot. It can come in handy for everything from controlled greetings with visitors, to encouraging settled behaviour for relaxation. Any type of negative association with the perimeter area will have the opposite effect and cause stress for the dog.

Checking In

Checking in is a natural progression from the previous impulse control lesson. This is a lesson that really needs to be taught in small steps, with gradual distractions.

As previously mentioned, many dogs check in as part of their natural relationship with their human. This is most obvious during walks, but like any other behaviour if it's not acknowledged or rewarded, it will stop happening and become extinct. As your dog is looking to you already, based on the previous lesson, all you need to do is mark and reward that look - with something the dog really likes, and practice within areas of manageable distraction until it can be carried out in a lot of different areas. You can do this with a marker and introduction of cue process, always using a motivational reward.

The only way you can run into trouble when teaching your dog that checking-in is the best choice, is by expecting too much too soon. In fact, raising distractions too quickly will provide your dog with more choices than he can manage, and make the choice you want him to practice far less likely.

In your living room at home, your dog is so used to the environment that focus on you if you are rewarding and motivational is easy.

If your dog checks in at home with no other choices, then you ask him to do it at the park where there are over a hundred sights, smells, sounds and stimuli you are taking his options from one to a million and his odds of getting it right larger than your odds of winning the lottery. You are setting him and yourself up to get it wrong. So, grow your distractions slowly and with care.

If your dog checks in with you naturally amongst more distractions than you have prepared him for, that's wonderful. Always mark and reward his initiative because he's making the right choice and rewarding it will prompt him to make the same choice again. Don't ask it of him though, until he is ready no matter what else is in the area.

The ultimate aim with this is that you can use the check-in on cue wherever you are, but also when carrying out the counter conditioning exercises later, you dog will learn to check-in naturally when he sees a potential trigger.

Important Note.

Some dog breeds and many insecure dogs are extremely visual and when they learn that checking in will get them a reward, they will offer the behaviour all the time. Whilst this may be great for your ego it's not so good for resilience and independent thinking for your dog. As much as possible, when the area is safe, and your dog can relax, it's important that he takes time to explore and enjoy the area. So, after checking in is learned and if your dog starts to become obsessive with you on walks, try not to reward every single check-in as this can restrict your dog's natural and relaxing independent behaviour.

Release

When your dog has learned to check in, you can prolong the eye contact by adding a release cue at the point you deliver the marker and reward. The release cue is especially useful for dogs that learn, think and act quickly – and that are onto the next thing as soon as they have achieved this task. Release is great for dogs that can become stressed quickly because if the dog is focussed on you, he has less chance of going down the route of making unhelpful choices.

Teaching the release cue is a case of gradually lengthening the time before delivering the final marker, if your dog struggles with that you can do a little continuous reward between the cue and release and gradually withdraw the interim rewards.

Generalisation

Impulse control and checking in with you are by far the two most important behaviours to teach at this point, if your dog is reactive to triggers. Successfully taught and generalised, these two behaviours will put your dog into a favourable position when he sees a trigger.

Whilst previously he may have seen a trigger and launched into a tirade of stay-away from me behaviour, or even more worrying, froze and gone into a state of emotional shutdown. When he has learned to make the two choices above, the dog will have the head space of his impulse control neural pathway, followed by the well-practiced choice of checking in with you for guidance.

For this reason, I class these two lessons as the first two that should be taught and generalised before anything else. There's little point having a dog that can sit on cue if he's likely to lose his mind when there's a stress trigger in the distance. Or a dog that can walk to heel perfectly but loses all focus and bond with you – unable to check in – if a trigger passes by on a walk. Everything else can be learned much more quickly when the foundations of mind space and the choice to check in first are laid.

Teaching these choices comes first and generalising them comes next.

Generalisation – sometimes called proofing, means that a dog is taught to make the best choice in all possible areas. Lack of generalisation would lead to a dog that can check in with you at home but is far too distracted to do it when you are outdoors. We generalise a behaviour in easy steps, doing everything we can possibly do to ensure that the right choice is the easiest one for the dog to make. So, we increase other options gradually and increase motivation to match.

To generalise a good choice, we must put ourselves in the dog's paws for a while, asking whether the changes for the environment for him are going to be easy or hard. Are the other options fair and will they use the same neural pathway for checking in with us or are they far too much of a distraction and set the dog up to make a poor choice in that moment (which would be anything other than checking in with us).

When he can make the choice to check in with you, add one or more other choices to the environment and balance the extra options with a higher motivation. If the difficulty goes up – the motivation should go up too.

Generalisation will include distractions, the amount of time the dog is asked to hold the choice and practicing in different areas until the choice is the dog's first one – no matter where he is. Distraction should ideally be introduced one at a time, within the dog's coping strategy, moving from the quietest to the busiest area in weeks as opposed to hours. Remember we are aiming for long-term foundational change, not a quick fix that falls apart later. So, we may start at home, then in the garden, the following week we go to a quiet field, then practice in different areas for a week and move onto a quiet park. Finally, we move to the busier parks, at the dog's pace.

The biggest problem you could run into here is doing too much too soon. Try to consider that the good choice is a tenacious neural pathway that needs much traveling on before it becomes established. In the same area there is another neutral pathway that is just as easy to take depending on the promise of a result. Your job is to keep your motivation the best possible result and to do this, you not only need to have an excellent motivator, but you also need to manage the environment as much as possible, to ensure a choice within it, is not more motivating than the one that you offer.

The most the good path is trodden, the more you can tweak the end of the second pathway, but you must always do it within the capacity of the dog!

Hand Press

Teaching your dog to press your hand with their nose is a form of basic targeting and can help with everything from calming to husbandry, for example – choosing to press their nose into your hand at the vets. Hand pressing is particularly good for dogs that are frustrated learners, because it teaches them to slow down. Touching is a brief and swiftly rewarded act and pressing is achieved by shaping the behaviour, whilst withholding the reward gradually.

The dog will learn the hand touch, before he learns the hand press. The hand touch is good for methodical learners because we can then use the hand as a target to get them moving around quickly, thus build their urgency and fun in the game. I taught my low confidence slow learner to hand touch, then practiced running around and offering him my hand as a target to chase– which certainly energised him and made him happy.

Targeting

Targeting is something that can be used time and again to grow persistence and healthy thought patterns. It can be used to bring enthusiasm to the dog that needs fun movement, to shape a choice – building confidence for the dog with low self-belief and to slow down the frustrated learner.

Whilst we are teaching a hand target here, anything can be a learned target, by using the same steps:

1. Have your marker and plenty of tiny treats.
2. Place your hand palm up and pop at tiny treat in the middle of your palm.
3. Offer the treat to your dog and the moment his nose touches your hand mark the touch and give your dog another treat - start adding your cue at this point.

4. Progress to mimicking putting a treat on your hand and start to mark the touch itself, then reward.
5. Practice with your hand in lots of different positions, always marking and treating the nose touch.
6. Bring your cue forward gradually – so use it earlier in the process.
7. Generalise the hand touch.
8. Whilst your generalising the touch, start to increase the time between cue and release. Do this at home first, remember we always teach new things in the blandest scenario.
9. Strengthen the hand press by gradually increasing the time and pressure by shaping it with your markers and rewards.

You can teach your dog to target his nose to your hand, a paw to your hand or even to rest his chin on your knee in the same way that you teach a nose press here. You could invest or make a target stick, teaching your dog to target to the end of it and use it to create movement and fun activities, which works particularly well for confidence building, as it's not too much to think about at once – plus it builds movement which makes the dog happy and willing to try new things.

Takeaway Points

- Walking a dog as a sole activity is likely to build their physical fitness rather than tire them out.
- Dogs need physical and mental stimulation to fully meet their needs.
- There is more than one learner type.
- Methodical learners take time to think before acting.
- A methodical learner may also lack confidence so need more encouragement and smaller lessons to build their self-belief.
- Frustrated learners will offer a repertoire of behaviours in the hope that they hit the right one.
- We should cater our coaching to the canine learner and bring our style of teaching in line with their capacity.
- Impulse control is the first lesson we teach – to practice mind space for the dog.
- Generalisation is necessary for all lessons but should be carried out at the dog's natural learning pace.

Chapter Nine

*"Dogs have more love than integrity.
They've been true to us, yes, but they
haven't been true to themselves."*
– Clarence Day

Fear

Emotional health is as important for dogs as it is for people. In some circles it's considered that dogs reach the emotional awareness of a small child, because they don't have the large frontal brain area of the adult human. There is currently minimal evidence of complex emotions such as guilt or shame, and other emotions associated with self-awareness.

Whilst we currently have no evidence of the domestic dog experiencing complicated emotional responses, they may, we just haven't proven it yet. We do know that dogs experience the basic survival emotion of fear.

Fear is an emotional response and one that changes behaviour. In fact, fear is one of the primary drivers of behaviour, because biologically it is linked with survival. To be scared is a completely natural response, yet it can become problematic for a variety of reasons.

The presence of fear in a dog's life is perfectly normal for survival. If a threat appears and is easily interpreted by the dog as a real threat, a healthy fear will help them to stay safe. For example, if the dog is in a field of cows and the cows give chase, the dog will experience a rush of adrenaline to get him out of there as quickly as possible, this is a helpful fear.

Innate fear to the occasional threat is normal, in fact it's healthy. Yet endless fear linked to stress or triggers that are unable to do the dog any harm, is detrimental to their quality of life and wellbeing.

There are three reasons that a dog may be naturally fearful, they can occur singly or as a mixture of two or three:

1. Genetic influence - if the dog's parents and grandparents have lived with fears all their life. Feral dogs for example, in some European countries may have an innate fear of people. That fear is highly likely to have been passed through generations. Epigenetic influence is genetic fear passed directly to the puppies through pregnancy and whelping. For example, puppy farm parents may have a healthy fear of the rough

people who keep them there and if they give birth then whelp their puppies in that environment – the puppies will inherit their fear.

2. If on the other hand the mother dog at conception was fetched into a kind and careful home, her stress during pregnancy and whelping may dissipate and the puppies may not inherit the same level of fear. Epigenetic inheritance will always prepare offspring for the environment the mother is in.

3. Fear is also caused by lack of positive social learning during critical periods. A dog that has poor quality or no social learning at all will fear new things. A young puppy that is passed around by a group of rough children in a state of fear, may not show that fear – but it will certainly show up in his behaviour later on. In the same way, a dog that grows up isolated from his own species altogether, may fear the ones he meets later in his life.

A trauma of any type can cause fear. It only needs to be one event. For example, my tiny puppy farm rescue Yorkshire Terrier was severely attacked by an off lead Jack Russell a few months ago. Whilst the only thing she hadn't previously feared was other dogs, she learned in that one traumatic event that dogs were scary too. She now sees another dog from outside of our home and goes stiff with fear.

Individuality will dictate how and even whether any dog becomes fearful, along with how they will react.

The fearful dog will always have behavioural symptoms, which show us their emotional state. The symptoms of fear are not identical though and will manifest in a way that is bespoke to the individual dog. The way that a dog responds to a trigger that they fear will depend on many things. Their stress levels, their breed, their learned behaviours, the situation and the exact environment. This includes trigger stacking and sensitisation.

Sensitisation means that the dog has become sensitised – over sensitive – to something specific. This could be a place, a trigger or something in the environment. A dog can be sensitive to anything at all.

We can split fearful reactions into three loosely defined groups:

1. Obvious fear - where the dog acts like they are scared. This is the flight or freeze reaction of the stress response and the dog stating that they want no trouble.
2. Frustration - not knowing how to behave or a reaction caused by a barrier to natural behaviour. This type of act can resemble aggression and a typical example is the dog that acts aggressively or impulsively on a lead or behind a gate, but not when the barrier is removed. Barrier aggression can escalate.

3. Fear Aggression - one of the most common forms of aggression and it's a totally natural response to a threat that will not retreat. Fear aggression is natural, and it can be practiced and learned, so that it becomes the default response to any perceived threat.

All the above reactions will be caused by one or more triggers.

Phobias

Phobias are classified as anxiety disorders. The dog that has a phobia of something specific will experience fear every time the object of their phobia is in the environment. The nature of phobic reactions varies and can seem irrational to the observer, but to the dog experiencing the phobia, the perceived danger is extremely real.

Fear and phobia are linked, and behaviour researchers Watson and Rayner tested this theory in 1920. They made their findings through another dubious experiment of the time, on a small (eleven-month-old) child.

The experiment was known as Little Albert. It was carried out by testing if a child could associate a white rat with a loud, scary noise. Initially Albert played happily with the rat, but then the scientists did as with Pavlov's bell, and introduced an unpleasant sound every time the boy reached to touch the rat. They created, in the child's mind, an unpleasant and distressing fear of the rat, a fear that then became generalised to items that closely resembled the rat. Their work was to show that phobias can be created, in the same way as pleasant expectations from the presence of a stimulus can be created.

The association was never reversed with Little Albert and it is believed he died aged six years old from illness. It is unknown whether he was still scared of items that he was conditioned to fear earlier in his life, at the hands of Watson and Rayner.

When the dog has learned to fear something, they develop a strategy for coping with it. Individuality dictates the level of fear that may be experienced, and how distressing the experience is for the dog. By observing behaviour, already discussed earlier in the book we can see how extreme the dog's fear or phobia is. As well as recognising their triggers and how quickly they go over threshold.

Fear Doors of the Mind

Dogs that become reactive to triggers have learned to fear something specific and created a go-to door in their mind of how to cope with that fear. This is their well-established neural pathway and it can be based on years of practice.

The object of the dog's fear will depend on the dog, the way that have learned to cope with it has probably been learned by trial and error and they have usually been conditioned - by life itself - to default to the same strategy for coping when scared.

Common triggers that dogs react to on walks or from their home and garden may include:

- Other dogs – all or those of a certain type.
- People – all or a specific gender or age, for example children.
- Moving objects such as cars or bikes.
- Sounds.
- Other animals.

Identifying a dog's triggers will take enlightened observation. In the beginning we may think that the dog is chaotic and reacts to anything and everything. It's easy to think this for two reasons:

1. The dog is highly aroused because he is trigger stacked, hypervigilant and ready to react within a split second.
2. The signals of stress are so frequent that it's difficult to find the start point in a behaviour change, therefore we can't associate an obvious change with an obvious trigger.

This may be the worst-case scenario and the dog in a continued state of hypervigilance will need some serious destressing before you begin the process that will be described in this chapter. We need the dog to be totally calm, to recognise and start working on getting them happy around the things that are causing them fear and stress. Before you begin, you may want to review the earlier description of the body language of a calm dog.

There are two terms we use for getting a dog used to things that he would normally fear. The first is counter conditioning and the second is desensitisation. Neither is less important than the other and ideally we would use them together, to produce the best results for the dog.

Systematic Desensitisation

Desensitisation is fundamentally based on classical conditioning (remember Pavlov's dog?). It is carried out by gradual exposure to a trigger, in a managed situation whilst the dog is relaxed.

Desensitisation is used in human psychology, in which case the subject is responsible for their own progress towards acceptance of the trigger. In human therapy the subject always learns how to relax themselves first with relaxing exercises and calming breathing exercises.

The therapy is then carried out as part of a hierarchy of fear – beginning with conscious thought about the trigger and working through to being in close proximity and finally touching/experiencing it. In this case the person gets to choose when they move between stages. They have the relaxation preparation and the choice to continue at a pace they can cope with.

In the same way we must create the relaxed state and choice for our dogs. We do this by first teaching relaxation then carrying out enlightened observation. We watch the dog's body language around the trigger. Then we adapt our own behaviour accordingly, the idea is that the pace he learns to accept the trigger at, is always decided by the dog. Carried out to perfection systematic desensitisation is subject led.

The use of desensitisation is best partnered with counter conditioning. So, we get the dog to a point where he can cope, by managing the distance from the trigger, then we introduce the favourable association with the trigger. The favourable association is usually food due to its power as a primary reinforcer. We will go through this in practical steps soon.

Counter Conditioning

Counter conditioning literally means changing how the dog has been conditioned to respond to a trigger, by creating a new association in the mind of the dog. It simply means creating a second association with the trigger – a positive one – that changes the way that the dog sees the trigger.

The dog's learning so far is termed conditioning. Your dog has been taught by the environment that something is scary and therefore a threat to his safety. This lesson may be completely senseless in your eyes but for your dog it's reality.

So, let's say for example that your dog fears big black dogs, and reacts to them every time he sees one. The big black dog is the trigger for your dog's fear. The behaviour strategy is your dog's reaction (which takes him directly to the Fear Door in his mind) and the whole thing is a conditioned response.

We can change most conditioned responses, and the good news is we don't even need to know the reason that the response became conditioned in the first place. We just need to consider the neural pathway that has become the dog's default choice when he encounters a trigger, then create a second more favourable one. We link this new pathway with a favourable choice and make it the easiest choice for the dog.

After a period of counter conditioning your dog sees his trigger - the large black dog - and he feels positive rather than fearful.

It sounds simple doesn't it? That's because it is quite simple but crucially it needs to be carried out from a foundation of calmness and only when the dog is way under threshold or it simply won't work. Any state of arousal will affect the dog's ability to learn, as we already know, so this lesson is all about space and timing.

Things to Avoid

We often hear people saying things like "they have to face their fears" or "dogs will sort it out amongst themselves" terms that can be used with persistence and authority. This is not something I would ever advise for dogs that are reactive based on fear and stress.

A technique which used to be common, but is thankfully not recommended anymore, is flooding. Used on people and dogs, flooding is the act of taking the subject over threshold and keeping them there until they calm down. There are many distressing ways that we still see this carried out in traditional dog training and none of them are good for the dog.

Force-based dog trainers still use flooding regularly. For example, within the alpha theory trainers still push scared dogs onto their side or back to show their authority over the scared dog, in an act that totally disempowers the dog, damages their ability to cope and is totally devoid of empathy.

When a dog is flooded because they are over-threshold, that dog believes they are in real danger. They think they are in a life and death situation and every system in their body is on full alert. This is a completely different state of mind and body to the dog that has been desensitised to their triggers systematically and learned that in fact triggers may lead to nice things too. The second dog is relaxed and empowered. The first needs at least three days to reach a basal relaxed state, is totally disempowered and has likely learned something else that he needs to be scared of.

Part of the reason that this approach has continued in the dog training world is that without looking at the results through knowledge, awareness and empathy it does seem to change the behaviour of the dog. The process will usually go like this:

The dog is scared and will try to avoid the trigger.

The closer the trigger gets, the more panicked the dog will become.

The dog reaches their threshold (an arousal level beyond their ability to cope) and they experience a fight, flight or freeze reaction. Fight may lead to barking at the trigger and trying to chase it away. Flight will be the dog showing typical fear response and trying to leave. Freeze will be shutdown physically and emotionally because the dog has learned that he cannot protect himself and must just accept what's coming.

The behaviour may be extreme – whichever route the dog's nervous system takes them on. It will then reach a point where the dog believes they are totally helpless, and they may appear to calm down – to the uneducated eye. This is really a form of overwhelm. The dog is emotionally and physically shut down and in essence, they have given up.

The dog that gives up in this way is at the other end of the wellness scale to a dog who has learned acceptance through relaxed counter conditioning. His distress is extreme, and the process has pushed him to his emotional limits.

So, whilst the behaviour may change in this case, the internal state has not changed – if fact it's probably even more distressed about the trigger than it previously was and that feeling will always resurface somewhere for the dog, because it's not been dealt with. The stress related to this treatment could even become physical illness.

This is why we never push dogs to face their fears. Instead we use positive and humane proven approaches, to teach the scared dog that there is a better choice and it's the most rewarding one that they can take.

Fear Aggression

No natural group animal will normally evolve with aggression as a central behaviour – because an aggressive animal is likely to be isolated from the group and isolation makes them vulnerable. An aggressive response during a scary experience is usually the last resort for a dog. As a social and group animal by nature, the dog will usually try a myriad of behaviours before believing that the only choice they have left is aggression.

As we have already explored, fear aggression is a matter of escalation for most dogs. They will go through a repertoire of communication until they feel that it is not working and then default to defensive aggression. If the dog learns that he can't escape via flight, he has no choice but to fight. This is a vitally important thing to remember with dogs that show defensive aggressive displays as default reactions whilst on the lead. The defence is usually learned because the dog has been unable to leave at some point.

As we know, all behaviours are linked with neural pathways and fear aggression is no different. The dog may have learned that the only choice they have is to become the aggressor when faced with their trigger. A few practices and the fear behind the behaviour may be invisible and we only see the aggression.

The pinnacle of aggression is the dog's bite. The damage that the bite does is based on the dog's threshold before they bite and how hard they bite.

Bite Threshold and Bite Inhibition

Bite threshold is the dog's biting point and how much the dog can cope with before they bite. The dog's bite threshold can change with the situation and their stress levels. Trigger stacking may lead to a low bite threshold to match the dog's high stress level, whilst the dog that is totally relaxed may have a very high bite threshold.

Bite inhibition is a learned process during puppyhood where a puppy learns to inhibit the strength of their bite to a force deemed reasonable. Learning bite inhibition is crucial for dogs, as any dog can be put into a position where they feel they need to bite. An inhibited bite will do far less damage than a dog who has not learned to inhibit the strength of their bite.

Important Note

All cases of regular or repeated canine aggression should be reviewed by the dog's veterinarian to rule out pain, biological contributors and possible illness. A veterinarian may even diagnose severe psychological distress and prescribe short-term medication. This can be extremely useful for some dogs when paired with effective and kind behaviour modification.

If you are reading this as a dog guardian and feel that your dog may be dangerous to yourself or others, it's vital to find experienced and quality professional support. Working with your own dog, whilst also having a strong emotional attachment to them and living together can naturally blindsight us to what is really happening.

Bringing in an experienced, objective observer that has spent time studying and learning about the canine species is vital in this case for making positive change. When seeking a professional, be aware that the industry is currently self-regulated and check methods along with certifications and study routes carefully.

As a canine professional it's vital to be honest with yourself when working with cases of aggression. If you believe that the problem you are dealing with needs more than your skillset currently offers, then seek help or refer to someone more experienced or qualified for canine aggression.

The good news is that even the most established fear aggression is an established neural pathway. With the right lessons and a carefully managed coaching environment, it can be changed for the better, teaching the dog a new way. By presenting a new choice than making it the default neural pathway to positive change.

Finally, behaviour modification for aggression should never trigger the behaviour, it will always keep the dog under threshold and move gently towards positive change, within the dog's capacity to cope. The lower the dog's arousal level is – the better they will learn and remember practice makes perfect.

Safety

In the next chapter we bring everything together in a carefully presented plan of action. There are some things that you can do now to lower the risk if a dog is highly stressed.

Safe-Space Triggers

Alongside preparing the dog to encounter and cope with his triggers outside the home it's also important to ensure there is no reason for stress within or at the direct borders of his home. If the dog that is worried about the outside world gets the opportunity, he may think he needs to watch that world, or listen carefully all the time for potential threats.

Any dog that is worried by the world can develop an anxiety about it, even when he's safe at home. So, sights, scents and sounds that invade the safe space will add to his anxiety.

Take some time to consider your home and how conducive it is to stress relief. Is your dog able to sit in the garden and bark at passers-by? Is the sofa pushed up to the window onto the street, giving a paranoid dog the freedom to watch for his triggers all day long? Or maybe your dog is more sensitive to sounds and your home is silent most of the time, leaving the dog in the uncomfortable position of needing to listen for the smallest sound in case it's a threat.

There are many ways to manage the behaviour if it's based in physical boundaries. For visual triggers you can frost the glass with a stick-on window sheet until the habit is broken. Perhaps move the room around so the dog doesn't need to worry about looking out of the window, something simple like a radio with soft music playing will bring the sound sensitive dog a lot of peace.

Management of a behaviour takes away the chance to practice it. If the environment is returned to its previous state, the behaviour is likely to return, but that depends on the dog and his circumstance. The important thing is that we ensure that home, the place where the stressed dog needs to feel safest, actually does feel safe for him and often it only takes a few enlightened, environmental tweaks.

Muzzle Use

Positive introduction of a muzzle will keep everyone safe. It will also prepare the dog for a muzzle if they ever need to wear one in an emergency.

There are a few muzzle types and they all have specific uses. The most important distinction to make is the difference between a muzzle for the vets which keeps the dog's mouth closed and one that is used for walking, which allows the dog to drink and pant as usual but removes the ability to bite.

A veterinary muzzle should never be used to muzzle a dog when walking. In fact, it should only be used for very quick treatments and removed as soon as possible. It works by holding the dog's mouth closed, to prevent biting, it also prevents breathing through the mouth and panting – which is predominantly how dogs lower their body temperature.

A box muzzle is the one used for walking and exercise. It's also called a basket or Baskerville muzzle. The dog is still able to carry out all normal behaviour in a box muzzle but cannot physically eat or bite. Many people shy away from muzzle use, however for the sake of the dog it's a good idea to create a positive association with the muzzle and if the dog is ever at risk of biting, a muzzle might be the best option.

Creating a positive association with a muzzle is carried out by targeting and positive reinforcement. First decide which muzzle you want/need to use, and this will be based on what it's needed for. Walking will require a box muzzle without fail. Preparing for vet visits will be fine with a veterinary muzzle that will only be on for a very short time.

After you have decided on muzzle type, pop it aside and get yourself a plastic or paper cup and lots of tiny treats. The cup should be big enough to fit the dog's nose in and enable them to get the treat. Then simply drop the treat into the cup and allow the dog to take it, mark the position of nose in cup and reward a second time. Repeat this a few times and then stop putting a treat in the cup and treat the *nose in* position as a targeting exercise. Add a cue and bring it forward as usual.

When the dog is happy to pop his nose in the cup to a cue, swap the cup for the muzzle and briefly go back to the first step, working through the others at the dog's pace. Taking the targeting to the point where the dog accepts a clipped-up muzzle may be a little tricky, but you can help the dog along by adding pate into a box muzzle and release the clip before the dog finishes licking then build the behaviour. For the veterinary muzzle, the pate is less of an option. Clipping the muzzle on and off whilst there is already a positive association will be easy, as long as you don't expect the dog to wear it for too long too soon. The biggest problem that can occur, but be avoided, is if you rush the process and the dog feels suddenly overwhelmed.

When you clip the muzzle on remember that you want the dog to be calm, so use a calming marker, when you take it off you can mark the end of the exercise with an exciting finale and use an exciting marker and a game, to cement the positive association with the exercise.

Walking Equipment

Walking equipment is varied and some of the collars and harnesses we see are best avoided. Generally, people that design walking equipment for dogs do it with one of two aims:

1. To benefit the human.
2. To benefit the human and the dog.

In the first category we see worrying collars and harnesses that make the dog uncomfortable but stop them pulling via the risk of being hurt. This can include prong and check chain collars, electricity and the use of harnesses designed to fasten around the dog's more vulnerable areas such as the soft stomach area. This type of equipment will suppress the dog's responses to the environment, but they won't feel any better in fact the threat of pain will make them feel much worse.

In the second group which is growing and ever improving is the walking equipment that makes the dog comfortable and helps the dog walker too. This is usually a harness that fits around the body well and is comfortable to wear. Sometimes if a dog pulls on the collar and lead, the introduction of a good harness will make an instant difference. Not always and most times the good quality harness and positive loose lead training will combine for excellent results.

For the dog that reacts with animated behaviour in the environment, walking equipment is particularly important. Repeated pulling on a collar can cause problems in the tender neck and throat area. Lunging and barking whilst wearing a collar is adding to the dog's unpleasant experience and may even be damaging them physically. By adding an uncomfortable collar to the dog that is already stressed, we can make them stressed even quicker. Even if the behaviour changes (through escape and avoidance) the dog's wellbeing is completely ruined.

Thankfully there are many excellent harnesses available now, that are comfortable for the dog to wear and evenly distribute the dog's weight, to prevent physiological issues. An excellent harness will be designed with the dog's well-being in mind.

If the dog's walking equipment is being changed to something more comfortable, the dog is likely to be relieved, particularly if a well-designed harness is used in place of a spiky collar. However, because dogs are individuals we can't assume that acceptance of the new equipment will be easy. So, from respect for the dog and with positive association in mind, we can carry out a targeting session to the new walk wear, just as we did the muzzle.

If you want to really empower the dog and have some fun along the way, why not try targeting the dog to wear the harness (just as we did to wearing the muzzle) then to retrieve the harness. Retrieving anything after targeting can be carried out by shaping the touch, the act of taking the item into the mouth, carrying it and finally retrieving it. Shaping in approximations means withholding your marker a little longer each lesson, until the dog can complete the final behaviour.

The dog that can successfully fetch his harness for a walk is starting the act of going outside with positivity and confidence, even before the walk begins.

It's wise to consider how you and your dog are physically attached to each other too. A training lead is essential, a soft material double ended lead that can be clipped at different lengths is easier and more comfortable than a pet lead. Flexi leads are best avoided for a number of reasons, they are hard to control if the dog is lunging, are easy to tangle yourself up in and they can offer a painful burn if they are pulled quickly against hand, legs or even other dogs.

A long line can be a useful training tool if you are confident to handle it and concerned about your dog's recall. The long line should be light, skin friendly and can trail on the floor behind the dog, easy to step on if needed. A long line needs to be used with a harness. To stop a dog in a collar, by stepping on a long line with be painful and can cause physical damage to the dog's tender neck and throat. If you do opt for this as a walking aid, practice with it around no triggers, you will be needing a fair amount of hand dexterity, when we start to work around triggers.

Takeaway Points

- Fear is an emotional state that drives behaviour.
- Innate fear of real threats is useful and related directly to survival.
- Reactivity is based on the fear of certain triggers.
- The dog's triggers for fear and their reaction to the triggers are based on the dog's individuality.
- Neural pathways determine how the dog reacts to their triggers.
- Fear aggression is a neural pathway to the way a dog has learned to cope.
- Aggressive behaviour needs professional help if the dog is a risk to himself or others.
- All dogs should learn to feel relaxed in a muzzle, even if it's just to alleviate their stress in an emergency.
- When a dog learns a positive association to a muzzle and walking equipment it empowers them and relieves their stress.
- Triggers inside the home need to be considered and managed to prevent stress in the place where the dog needs to feel most safe.

Chapter Ten

"Old dogs, like old shoes, are comfortable. They might be a bit out of shape and a little worn around the edges, but they fit well." – Bonnie Wilcox

Feeling Safe Outdoors

This area of the book seeks to bring together everything we have covered to carry out successful and positive behaviour modification. We aim to build the dog's resilience and empower them to make the right choices, in managed environments – helping the dog to learn that he can cope in the world, and even enjoy it.

There are many things that we can consider truth for every dog. For example, dogs are group animals and isolation can affect their well-being. The dog is also a domesticated animal so whilst he once lived in a group of his own kind, we are in many cases now his peers.

There are also things that we need to consider totally unique to every dog and this will always be the first step in any behaviour modification program.

Genetic and biological factors to behaviour.

A dog's personality is in part shaped by the DNA passed down from his parents and grandparents. If we research the breed type or types in any individual dog, we will learn things that help us to understand them as an individual.

This is a vital part of background knowledge for every dog. Genetic inheritance will show us not only why the dog reacts to triggers in the way that he does but also how we can best motivate him for positive changes. When dealing with any dog, the first step to take is getting to know the history of the breed, the role that they were originally bred to fulfil and any behaviour tendencies that may occur.

Explore a good range of reference sources to obtain this information. The more knowledge you have of the breed or breed types, the better you will understand the motivations and behaviour strategies of the individual dog. Gathering information is paramount to understanding, for example we can consider the following genetic influence for a specific breed of dog:

- Breed type.
- Original role.
- Behaviour associated with that role.

- How that behaviour may manifest in domestic life.
- How the behaviour can become problematic in domestic life.
- How the dog copes when aroused.
- Motivation - things the dog likes based on artificial selection.
- How we can use that motivations to change behaviour.

If I were to fill this out for one of my own dogs, it would provide me with the following information, before I even see the behaviour in action.

Chips is a rescued Jack Russell Terrier cross of eight years old.

- Jack Russel Terrier.
- Ratting and hunting.
- Boldness, independence and loyalty to handler. Digging, barking and confidence to confront small animals, even when sent down rat or rabbit holes.
- Barking, boldness and independent thinking.
- Barking at triggers, defensive and aggressive displays when scared.
- Copes by trying to look scary and bigger than the threat – a strong display of confidence.
- Motivated by toys, play, interaction with handler. Motivation by food as a primary reinforcer.
- Object play to trigger dopamine, bond building with handler, teach choice for handler interaction.

This set of information is a pretty accurate description of Chips. The only thing it doesn't cover is that Chips is most likely a cross breed and the smaller part of his genetic inheritance is not obvious. By getting to know him I can observe more about his personality, which shows a sensitive nature, tinged with anxiety which is the foundation for all the behaviours above.

Now let's consider another dog breed, who has a very different nature altogether:

- German Shepherd Dog
- Herding and more recently guarding.
- Protective behaviour with warnings and confidence to follow through.
- Protecting the handler. Reacting to triggers with aggressive displays of warning.
- Guarding the handler.
- Barks and counter-threatens the threat.
- Motivated by handler interaction, motivated by food as a primary reinforcer.
- Trigger dopamine with food and full attention to offer the choice of handler interaction as opposed to handler protection.

This list is the first step towards understanding the innate responses and motivations of any individual dog. If you are reading with a specific dog in mind, take some time to apply the list to them. Whilst mine is brief, you may want to add much more to your own for the purposes of growing your own knowledge and understanding, particularly if you work with dogs on a professional basis.

Even if the dog's learned behaviour seems to overshadow their genetic tendencies, they will be there, and the information will help. If we know what a dog's genes might dictate they like best, we are enlightened to greater possibilities for motivation.

Try to think beyond the usual toys, games and food for motivation, remember that each dog has preferences and they will be unique to him. I once trained a hearing dog for a deaf lady by trawling the charity shops for soft toys that made unusual noises. There was little confidence or motivation for food but if he could gently hold a noisy toy at the end, that little dog was willing to learn anything.

Stress Relief

Now we have recognised who the dog is and what he likes best, let's consider one of the biggest parts of this process – decompression. Any dog that has spent some time stressed and worried about life, or repeatedly exposed to his triggers will need to decompress before he is at the point where effective learning is possible.

The aim at this point of the process is to identify what exactly relaxes the dog and apply those things to his life for a while, maybe even in the long term. There are many ways that we can relax our dogs and it's just a case of finding the right one for every individual dog.

A specific room in the house might be relaxing. Perhaps the bedroom or a place where the dog can go to hide from the world for a while. If there's nothing available that's suitable you could create a safe space with a suitably sized crate and a blanket over it that the dog can retire to. As with all positive changes, get creative. We have an alcove fireplace in our dining room that is rectangular, so we have a big dog bed and blanket tucked in there and there's always at least one dog in it.

Provide some audio relaxation. There are many free soundtracks and music loops that are created with the aim of canine relaxation. You can find them free online or purchase them for home use. Music has the extra bonus of drowning out external noises and it's possible to see your dog visibly relax when the music goes on, if the sounds suit him.

Offer physical relaxation. The right kind of touch is a very effective route to relaxation if the dog is comfortable with being handled and touched physically. A basic, light massage is a great way to settle a dog who loves to be touched, start at the ears as they have many nerve endings and work gently down your dog's body to the tail. It's lovely to help a dog to physically relax in this way, if it suits them. The right dog will really appreciate a light massage.

TTouch similarly has excellent results for relaxation. The idea of this method is to gently massage the areas of the dog's body needing stimulation for gentle energy movement. If you are interested in trying this method there are lots of free videos online, just ensure you use a reputable source.

Physical relaxation can be taken a step further by teaching the dog specific postures and stances that encourage them to slow down and be relaxed within their body. The advantage of this approach is that it improves energy flow, by slowing the dog down and it also improves mind space because the dog learns to wait in position for the next cue.

Slowing down with postures must consider the dog's physiological health. For example, a dog with hip or back problems must not be taught postures that exacerbate pain or injury.

Postures can be taught using shaping with a marker. Stepping the two front paws onto a yoga block and holding the position until release is a good example to slow the dog down and give them mind space. When the dog has learned to do the two front feet, you can teach the opposite and shape the same behaviour with the two back feet raised on the block. Remember not to ask the dog to hold the position for longer than he's capable at that point. A broken position is the start of a new neural pathway, an unhelpful one. If you feel adventurous you could teach your dog to bow on cue, a posture the stretches out the spine and body, for relaxation.

Any posture taught at home can later be retaught in the environment. The dog that already knows the cue will benefit greatly from repeating the coaching steps anyway. Re-learning in a different environment puts the dog in the mind-set of success and, "bingo I can do this".

Scatter feeding is an excellent relaxation exercise, for best results use small and tasty food that needs effort to find, the grass is a good place to scatter food, or wrapped in an old towel.

Scentwork for fun is also a great way to relax your dog at home for a while, without going into the scary world. Playing with and then hiding a toy (or hiding food) in increasingly complex places will use up a lot of the dog's energy and help them relax during and afterwards.

Dogs have an amazing ability with scent and to use it will use their body and mind in a way that leads to extra relaxation.

The Dog's Nose

The average dog has 220 million olfactory receptors in his or her nose. This is a huge amount, when we compare it to the average six million within the human nose.

The extra receptors make a dog capable of differentiating between scent in greater detail, which is the reason dogs can smell more variation of scent and why they can smell tiny amounts of a chemical. As a dog is so reliant on his nose, the nose itself has evolved to be totally efficient, to the point that the soft tissue inside the nasal area can accommodate both air and scent, yet still differentiate between the two well enough for the dog to recognise even the smallest scent.

It is the dog's separation within the nasal cavity which quickly allows scent and air to go separate routes within the body, immediately after the point of inhalation. When this happens, the air goes into the lungs and around the circulatory system to oxygenate the cells and keep the dog healthy. The scent goes up towards the olfactory receptors and the olfactory bulb that deals with scent, at the front of the brain.

The dog exhales through the slits at the side of his nose rather than pushing the air back out directly through his nostrils which would also push out any incoming scent. This leaves the dog able to continually draw in scent through his nostrils and up towards his brain on a constant basis.

With all this happening during even the most relaxed and fun scentwork enrichment sessions, it's unsurprising that dogs really enjoy sniffing for fun – and they it becomes a great prelude to proper rest.

Walking

Whether you rest your dog for a day or a week depends on how stressed he was in the beginning of the process and how quickly he relaxes. Walks should be re-introduced as carefully as possible to avoid uncontrolled triggers in the environment.

It's best to aim for a quiet place, with as little stimulation as possible when re-introducing outdoor walks. Otherwise you run the risk of pushing the dog's stress levels right back up and undoing all the hard work you have put in. The good news is you can gradually increase exposure in a controlled way that your dog can cope with and that will grow his long-term resilience.

Behaviour Identification

You probably already have a good idea about your dog's triggers, those things that send him over the edge. It's important to view everything with a fresh perspective now as it will give you all the information you need about how the world currently affects your dog and how you can help him. Try to maintain a relaxed state of mind yourself too, breathing exercises and general mindfulness will help with this.

We tend to live in a mindless world where most of us are thinking about something else a lot of the time. We can change that though by spending some time just being present in our minds. This can be achieved by focusing on your breathing for 10 deep breaths – this will oxygenate your brain and bring you back to full mindful focus. Practice it a few times a day and make it a habit. Then take your new habit out on walks with you. It will keep you calm, use your observation skills and keep your mind from wandering during this important process.

Within behaviour modification we consider three steps to maintenance of a behaviour. What triggers the behaviour, how the behaviour is displayed and what comes directly after the behaviour. We can consider this process in the same way if we swap the term behaviour with the word choice.

So, in the past your worried dog may have been startled by the presence of a trigger; for example, another dog on a lead and made a choice to react. That choice could have been to bark at the other dog who then coincidently moved away – simply carrying on with their walk and your dog immediately believes that their own act sent the other dog away. There we have an example of a choice that your dog believes worked for him, which makes him more likely to carry out the same choice again. The choice is reinforced by the consequence. If the choice is practiced enough to create a neural pathway fuelled with high arousal, it can create an extreme reactive behaviour.

Another example would be the dog that barks at cars that pass in the street. The dog reacts because he fears the noisy moving object, the object is the trigger for his fear and the consequence the dog associates with his choice is that the car gets further away. The fact that a car retreats quickly when a dog barks at it, is a perfect consequence for that dog and has totally reinforced that choice.

Triggers

The trigger(s) for your own dog's reactive behaviour are the things that cause stress or fear in him. Triggers are completely limiting to your dog's life and quite limiting to your own life too. If, before the decompression period, your dog was reacting overtly to his triggers he was doing so for one of the following two reasons:

He had learned that the trigger came closer or he got closer to it – even when he tried to communicate his discomfort. So, he has learned to bypass the subtler ways of communicating and chosen to move directly onto something more overt.

He was showing the signs of discomfort and they went unnoticed, so his behaviour escalated. He felt he had no other choice.

Both points are associated with arousal beyond the dog's ability to cope, that have taken him over his own personal stress threshold, into the realms of his natural need to fight, flight or freeze. We must remember that this is not within his control. The good news is that following decompression, we now have a dog who is relaxed and the knowledge of those early signs that the dog is uncomfortable. These two things will help us to turn the walk into a well-managed exercise in growing resilience.

On the first few walks try to set your dog up for success by visiting a quiet, open field which has lots of space for escape.

The plan is to use the area for observing your own dog and responding to his acknowledgement of triggers in the distance.

Try to avoid:

- Pathways with boundaries or where your dog has to walk directly up to and past another dog. This is a very unnatural approach and will trigger fear and probably a choice to react.
- Places where there is lots of stimulation at peak time, for example urban parks during the school holidays or at the end of the school day.
- Places where loose dogs may run up to your own dog and take him over threshold before you have chance to get him to safety.
- Dog parks.
- Areas with lots of tourists.

This doesn't mean you need to avoid these areas forever (which you may have had to without building your dog's resilience). It just means that you can visit them when you and your dog are ready and when his resilience is raised enough for him to cope.

A Safe Bubble

Your dog has an area around him which we will call his bubble. It's based on the flight distance that we discussed earlier. The size of his bubble will be unique to your dog and his view of the world. The dog is right at the centre of his bubble all the time and monitors the edges of it carefully.

If a dog reacts to other dogs at great distance, then his bubble will be large and the edges of it will spill into areas far away. If he only reacts when others come within five metres, your dog has a smaller bubble and can cope with others in the distance better but his reaction to dogs that enter his personal space is no less severe than the dog with the bigger bubble.

So, let's imagine that your dog's bubble is ten metres from edge to edge. This means he has five metres to the front, behind and to his left or right before he feels stressed and reacts. This can work perfectly, in an ideal world where the space is open, and you can see for thirty metres each way.

Safety bubbles, like normal bubbles, respond to the environment though and they will change shape if the environment dictates it. So, if you choose to walk on a footpath with side boundaries, your dog's bubble will respond accordingly.

The bubble will most certainly cover the same space, but the dog will naturally redistribute where that space is. So rather than the easily manageable five metres in every direction, the bubble will become long and thin because the boundaries dictate it. The dog may then only have a metre to each side of him, and yet the front and back safe space will expand greatly. This means he will react to a dog that approaches from ahead at a much greater distance than five metres. He does this because the head-on approach is intimidating, and the bubble has changed shape to suit the environment.

The dog's safe bubble is where you do your work together when out in the environment. The aim is to keep him within that safe space and always keep his boundaries intact. Anything that comes into that space will cause a reaction but if we can keep the bubble intact, with quick thinking, the bubble will naturally shrink over a short amount of time and your dog will become much more relaxed.

To establish the size and nature of your dog's safety bubble you can use enlightened observation. Watch carefully for signs that your dog is starting to feel uncomfortable, for example he's suddenly focussed on something that has moved closer, or he's showing signs of low level stress. When this happens, your dog's bubble is in jeopardy and if you don't re-establish his safe space, your dog will very quickly make his default choice and react defensively.

There will be real-life situations where loose dogs run up to you and it's a real problem in general. It's a good idea to plan your initial walks in places or at times where other dogs are a minimum at the beginning. As your dog's resilience grows, so will his ability to cope with other dogs. You may want to invest in a lead or coat that states your dog needs space. It's also a good idea to practice a swift 90 degree turn and sprinkling small treats on the ground in the bushes to keep your own dog happy whilst others pass. We can never account for the people who don't or can't recall their dogs. A sharp and loud "call your dog" can work wonders. Whilst we can't avoid people who won't recall their dogs completely we can do our best by good planning and excellent preparation to deal with others in the area.

The First Walk

Skills required at this point are a sharp eye and a quick response. Tools are a lot of small treats, your dog's toy if he likes them and a positive attitude.

Your first task is to scan the area for potential triggers. Anything that your dog has reacted to in the past is likely to be a trigger, but anything at all in the environment is a potential trigger. Ideally you will mentally risk assess everything you see; the loose dog in the distance, the bike on the road or the mother with a screaming child in a pushchair heading your way.

When you identify a potential trigger, watch your dog carefully for signs of unease. Common low-level signs of unease include lip licking, focus on the potential trigger or a cut-off signal where your dog glances away then back at the trigger. It's a good idea to go back to the earlier chapter on communication as a recap on all possible signs.

If your dog shows even the smallest sign of unease at this point it's time for you to spring into action and get him further away from the thing he is focussed on. You may only need to take two or three steps away and give your dog a treat, for the unease to disappear. You may need to go much further.

Use this walk to simultaneously maintain your dog's safe space in the environment and engage with him on lots of relaxing activities. We are creating new neural pathways not only for behaviour but also for expectation. To this point your dog may have expected a world fraught with danger on walks, now we want him to expect a well-maintained safe space, the opportunity to relax and the ability to make some good choices that lead to success.

Whether you have your dog on or off lead for this walk is decided completely by your dog and your individual situation. Many dogs that react are better off the lead because it gives them the freedom to escape. However, this is only advisable with dogs that have excellent recall. You could choose off lead, on lead or a long-line for this first walk, always remember though - safety first!

This walk should be a mix of exploration and interaction. Let the dog sniff and explore the area as this is a natural act that all animals are entitled to practice. Reward any check-ins (looking at you), practice impulse control with a treat or toy and re-teach something that you have already taught at home.

Play, then encourage another relaxing explore and head for home.

Repeat this type of walk a few times at least. Remember we are teaching the dog that the outside world is a nice place to be, that his safe space is indeed safe. You are getting him in the frame of mind to learn to cope with his triggers. If your dog's safe space is broken by a loose dog or another trigger at this point, don't be disheartened. Just do your best to maintain his space - help him relax again and move on.

Engagement is vital. When you and your dog work together on something, such as a game or task you are fully engaged with each other. This can slip in everyday life and lead to a dog feeling ignored, which leads to bad choices – one of those is reactivity. Remember that we are aiming to make the best and healthiest choice, the easiest one for the dog to make.

Engaging with your dog throughout these walks is crucial. Even if you only go out for twenty minutes, split your time into five-minute blocks for example:

- Independent exploration and sniffing at the dog's own pace.
- Re-teaching a cue.
- Play or sprinkled food.
- Independent exploration and sniffing at the dog's own pace.

Ideally after the first few walks, even with the odd unplanned introduction, your dog should be much more relaxed in the environment and in general. His behaviour and body language should be loose most of the time, his confidence should be high, and he should be checking in with you regularly on walks. When the same level of relaxation on uninterrupted walks – as the dog has at home- is achieved we can move onto systematic desensitisation and counter conditioning for positive change.

This part of the process may disrupt your life somewhat but it's important to remember that in comparison to a lifetime of living with reactive behaviour and your dog being stressed, two or three weeks of adapted walks is favourable. Even if you walk at six in the morning so you can have the fields to yourself – remember it's only to set new foundations that you can build behaviour change on. Most importantly, it will lead to a much better future for both of you and won't be forever.

Walking & Working

This is the point that we begin moving the newly relaxed dog back into the world that stressed him, and we do it with care and management. Depending on how quickly your dog has learned to relax outside, will dictate when you start this part of the process.

Your dog's capabilities and potential will be paramount here. It's vital to remember that we are building a strong neural pathway and simultaneously eradicating an established one that has so far been linked to negative emotion.

Working with Triggers

Only when your dog is relaxed will we begin working with triggers again, by actively using systematic desensitisation and counter conditioning.

The task is to manage the environment as well as possible and to observe your dog for any changes in their relaxed state. Burn into your mind's eye the symptoms that your dog feels uneasy, then use that knowledge to ensure your dog doesn't go over threshold at any point.

Keeping Your Distance

With a relaxed dog and a well-chosen area, you can practice walking at a manageable distance from triggers. Remember the dog's bubble and maintain the safe distance, always. The aim is to get your dog used to the triggers at a distance he can cope with whilst also providing a good experience at the same time.

At this point you will need to let go of any self-consciousness and focus on your dog. Choose an area where you can carry out real-life set ups at a reasonable distance to anyone else in the area. You will almost certainly find yourself changing direction a lot in the beginning – because you will be moving in response to how your dog feels at the time.

As with all coaching, you must set your subject up to succeed and you can do that by bringing a specific coaching session into your walks at this point.

Start with relaxation then take your dog a little closer to his triggers, relax again, then triggers again then relax and home. When you take your dog near his triggers it's vital that you keep his safety bubble intact and at the point he is closest to the scary thing (which shouldn't be very close at all) you introduce the counter conditioning reinforcer. Food as a reinforcer for counter conditioning is excellent.

On or Off Lead

Whether you have your dog on or off the lead at this point is based on your dog's recall and likelihood to run at the trigger if it gets too close - or come back when called. On and off lead reactivity should be viewed on an individual basis, for the dog and his capacity.

Grisha Stewart when defining her Behaviour Adjustment Training technique discovered that dogs find the act of moving away from the trigger, a functional reward. Meaning that the act of increasing distance is rewarding and as BAT training is based on the dog's choices, giving the dog the option to move quickly away from the trigger – for a functional reward gives an extremely successful result. This is excellent when we can be sure that the dog is below the reactivity threshold and has quick results. However, if your dog is likely to run at the trigger, with attack as a form of defence, it's worth having them on the lead, at least until you can be sure how he will act with triggers in the distance. You can still move quickly away from the trigger, it just means you do it together.

Similarly, if your dog doesn't have a reliable recall, don't take the risk of introducing triggers and the option of running at them, until you are certain that he won't.

How a dog reacts to his triggers is like any other behaviour – based on his personality and prior experiences. Some believe that the only choice they have is to rush forwards towards the trigger, whilst others would choose to move away. Rushing towards the trigger is a habit that is based on a neural pathway, it may have worked or been reinforced in the past and it's the dog's easiest choice at the time.

Most dogs learn to rush at the trigger from having a few experiences where they have felt there was no other choice. For example, walking towards another dog on a path, as a direct approach with no other obvious option – will lead to practice of this act. The dog's choices (in his fearful mind) are to be the aggressor or the victim. Another way that a dog can learn to rush up with hostile intent is by practicing barrier frustration on the lead for so long that when they are off lead, the frustration just takes them directly to their trigger.

Neutralising the direct approach effect is necessary and now you have the tools to do it, you can change the walking environment, or simply turn around and walk away.

It's a good idea to teach a quick direction change on cue before you begin step one – something simple like "this way" and as you change direction and your dog joins you, add a reward. Soon your dog will be changing direction on cue and as soon as they hear the word(s) they will be thinking about turning and walking away, for their reward. The quicker you spin and walk away, the less likely your dog is to focus on the trigger.

Even when a direct approach is inevitable, often due to off lead dogs that are not recalled, you can use a little scatter feeding at the side of the path. You can also use the cues we taught earlier, encouraging your dog to check in for a reward, or hand touch on cue. If another dog does run up, or look like he may, turn and walk away as quickly as possible. If your dog goes over threshold, don't worry too much – all the work you are doing will ensure he copes better than he did before so just raise your stress busting for a couple of days and carry on.

Neutralising barrier frustration can be carried out in the same way. The trick with this is not to allow focus on the trigger at this early stage, for any amount of time. Focus will lead to raising stress levels and directly to that same unhelpful choice that your dog has been practicing for some time. When you begin the steps below, check-ins will start occurring naturally and then you must quickly reinforce them.

Eventually with careful coaching all dogs should realise they don't have to run at the 'threat' but they can just stay calm and move away – yet still stay safe.

A Positive Association

Whilst a marker after a couple of sessions will do the job, the first sessions of counter conditioning to a trigger – at manageable distance – should have a highly positive effect!

The reward at this stage should be something super tasty that makes the dog feel like seeing the trigger is the best thing in the world. In addition, it should be slightly difficult to obtain, for example a chew stick that the dog can break bits off but not take entirely, or a squeezy tube of soft cheese. The idea behind this is to reinforce the new neural pathway by keeping the dog's mind on the reward for as long as possible by prolonging the reinforcement. A quick swallow will send the dog's mind right back to the trigger in split seconds. Ideally your dog will see the trigger and try to obtain the food at the same time.

When the above is achieved – swiftly move further away from the trigger. This completes the positive association, and keeps the dog relaxed.

If your dog's behaviour starts to change when they see the trigger at this early stage, you are too close or have held the position for too long. It's possible to do one or both these things and either will be detrimental to counter conditioning. The first sign of the dog's stress levels rising is often focus on the trigger, swiftly losing the inclination to be distracted, then the reinforcer will stop being attractive and the dog has started down the route of their reactive choice. An easy way to tell if your dog is stressed by a real-life situation is whether they will take a usually favoured treat after the event. My little Yorkie loves food but when a loose, strange dog has approached her, she refuses it, right until her stress levels dissipate.

You are likely to see this from your dog at some point during this process, just as your dog is learning, so are you. There are real life circumstances outside of our control and even the chance of misjudging situations which lead to the dog making the old choice – but that's OK if you're doing your best and learning from it, then it's working. The trick to learn is that distance neutralises stress, so if you see any signs that the dog is about to show a fearful or stress based reaction, move quickly and calmly away from the trigger – to neutralise their stress and return to their basal relaxed state.

Practice taking your dog within sight of many variations of his triggers and rewarding him for relaxed behaviour. Remember that you must set-up the situation so that he stays relaxed. This process is the first step to establishing the new and healthier neural pathway, which will be his future choice when faced with something that once scared him enough to react.

By the end of step one you should have the confidence and ability to recognise the current edge of your dog's personal safety bubble, keep it secure and practice the cues we learned earlier, with your dog's triggers in the background. Your dog should have the ability and knowledge that you will keep him safe. The triggers mean something good is going to happen and that checking in with you is the most rewarding choice he can make.

By this point walks should be a more relaxing experience, packed with an even balance between relaxing in the environment and interaction with you. All the time the triggers will be in the background – not at the centre of everything like they once were.

Parallel Walking

Step two of this process is making the bubble smaller. This can happen surprisingly quickly when managed carefully. It can be tempting to do too much too soon or even assume that if your dog has been close to his trigger once and not reacted, then he's fine to do that same again. Remember though, that all situations are different, and your dog is learning something completely new here.

Imagine that your dog's learning is based on a journey – which in many ways it is – his journey through life. Try to imagine that every choice between relaxed behaviour or a reactive response is a fork in the road. One route is well-established whilst the other is new and infrequently trodden. The road travelled to that fork may have been a relaxing route, or it could have been fraught with stressors (triggers). The route so far will determine which road the dog takes at the fork and if he's feeling optimistic and confident – he's way more likely to try the new route. However, if the dog feels insecure and stressed, he's most likely to take the route he knows well because he will naturally seek familiarity, in times of trouble.

Your task is to manage the journey and manipulate the road as much as possible, so that your dog experiences a relaxed ride, by building his resilience and self-belief, ensuring that he has the confidence and positive expectation to make new choices every step of the way.

Reducing the size of the bubble will be easier in steps. If your dog is worried about other dogs you will both benefit from taking him to the current edge of his bubble – as close to another dog as he can be whilst staying relaxed – and walking parallel on leads whilst reinforcing relaxed behaviour all the way.

Ideally the other dog will be steady, easy going and relaxed. They will show little interest in your own dog at this point, as even positive interest can be intimidating to a scared dog. If you can set this up with a suitable dog, do that, because it will make the situation way more manageable if you can communicate directly with the other dog's handler. It's important to consider your dog's exact triggers here too, for example if your dog fears big black dogs, you may want to start with another breed. Or if that's not possible, at a slightly bigger distance.

If you can't find or don't know a dog for set-ups, all is not lost. It's possible to do managed set-ups by picking a suitable looking passer-by in the park and discreetly walking parallel with them for a short time.

Always watch your dog's body language and behaviour, look for those early signs of tension and increase the distance. Only decreasing it again when your dog has relaxed.

There's a trap that it's possible to fall into at this point, which it's important to be aware of. It can be easy to take your dog too close to the trigger and notice that they have become tense, yet then try to walk parallel with the trigger dog – however, this will be counter-productive. Always remember the desensitisation is systematic and works for exactly that reason. If the dog's body language becomes tense it means that their stress reaction has begun, which is exactly what we are trying to leave in the past.

If this step goes well your dog will be checking in with you regularly, he will know that the other dog is there but will soon relax and get on with his own choices. This is excellent progress – even if a dog could previously walk alongside another yet was on edge all the way, the relaxed behaviour is an amazing achievement for their well-being.

End each session of decreasing the size of the dog's safety bubble by moving further away from the trigger and carrying on with the walk. This way it becomes a normal part of the walk. Never rush step two. A dog may have learned to fear something over the course of years. Decreasing a safety bubble over three or four sessions is absolutely possible for some dogs, in the right situation with the right set-up, but for many it will take a few more sessions.

Consider your dog's position as one where the environment will dictate his choices every step of the way. Ask yourself not what he's going to do, but which choice he's likely to make and why. For example, the big black dog passing by might lead to a crossroads where option one for your own dog may be to defend via a reactive display, or option two may be to go the other way with you and receive positive reinforcement for making that choice. For your dog, both options lead to the same underlying desired result – no forced approach from a scary trigger.

Yet if the option to go the other way isn't obvious, your dog has lost the healthy choice and will most certainly default to option one. Or if the approaching trigger is too close – into their safety bubble – your dog will experience fight or flight and default to option one, believing it's his only choice. This is exactly why we need to look at the dog's opportunity for choices within the environment well before he is forced to make them.

Step two may be all you need to get to with your own dog. Introduced and managed carefully it will create a different experience on walks Your dog will be relaxed enough to cope with triggers because his safety bubble has decreased in size and he has learned to choose to move away from them. The odd occurrence of stressful event will not affect him like before because your dog's resilience is higher than it's ever been.

Another reason that you may want to stop at step two is if your own dog is aggressive towards his triggers and you believe that it won't benefit him to introduce greetings. Sometimes, based on a traumatic history, dogs simply don't want to be around other dogs – or they bond with dogs in their family but have no interest in building relationships or interaction with unknown dogs. This is another situation where our dogs should have the opportunity to choose. We may want them to play or like other dogs, but they might want something different altogether and we should respect that.

Set-ups can be carried out for all triggers, not just dogs. Another example of a trigger is children. They move oddly and make a lot of strange sounds, which can be scary to a dog that has never been socialised to them. It's a good idea to ask someone with a sensible child to help with step two if you can, as following unknown kids around the park can lead to all sorts of problems. Plus of course, children are as inquisitive as puppies, still learning themselves and will often directly approach a dog – if he's barking at them or not. It's a good idea when setting up step two with a child and their adult to have the child quiet at first then introduce sounds, chattering and even shouting, as your dog learns to cope. This will prepare your dog for real life situations and all the noises that children tend to make naturally.

Greetings

Step three of the process is to facilitate greetings if your dog will benefit from them. Meet and greet between dogs that don't know each other needs to be carefully handled regardless of the situation. Just as people get first impressions from other people, dogs learn a lot about another dog and whether they want to interact with them, from that first few seconds of the encounter.

As we already know, well socialised and socially capable dogs greet and interact with each other via a series of carefully delivered and shared communication signals. We also know that there are many dogs that can't greet politely, that fear their own species or that misread the signals of others. This is largely due to lack of social learning.

Greetings between unknown dogs must be carried out safely, considering the communication, choice and the feelings of both dogs involved. We must always avoid the things that cause reactive choices, so we never walk directly up to one dog on the lead – with another dog on the lead, as this can be intimidating for even the most confident dog, and downright scary for the others.

On lead interactions can occur but only for super relaxed dogs that show no signs of barrier frustration. A three second sniff with plenty of loose lead is a suitable greeting and they must take place through walking closely parallel, as opposed to face on. Watch out for tension, a hard stare or posturing from either dog, as that could spell trouble.

Managing arousal in greeting is extremely important. Dogs that are highly aroused and that race up or even approach with obnoxious submission are unpleasant to encounter for most worried dogs.

Similarly, one of the reasons that dogs show reactive behaviour towards other dogs – or anything at all – is over arousal. Therefore, greetings must take the same approach that we have focussed on throughout the book, the dog must be at their natural state of calm and be relaxed. Every step closer to their trigger should only be taken when the dog is calm. By taking the dog too close, too soon, we would be running the risk of taking the dog over threshold.

Use enlightened observation and the canine communication that we learned earlier in the book, to be sure that the greeting is going well. You will find added illustrations in the resources area of this book, to help you recognise calming signals, fear and anxiety in dogs.

Remember that your dog is relying on you to keep him safe, when you do his trust will grow.

Just as we have covered reactive behaviour towards other dogs here, the same process can be followed when building resilience to any trigger at all. This final part is simply a change of association to something. When the foundations of relaxation and resilience are laid, desensitisation and Counter Conditioning will be the final, successful step to a healthier future.

Takeaway Points

- Knowledge of a dog's breed type will keep us informed of the dog's reaction style and how we can motivate him.
- Practicing mindfulness will help you throughout the coaching process.
- Every choice the dog makes can become an established behaviour based on what happens before it, what the behaviour is and what happens directly after it.
- The consequence that a dog associates with his own behaviour will drive a repeat of the behaviour.
- Every dog has a safety bubble which is completely individual and responds to the environment.
- Triggers outside the safety bubble will not result in reactive behaviour.
- Triggers that come inside the safety bubble will cause reactive behaviour.
- The first few walks are vital for teaching relaxation in the environment via the avoidance of triggers and varied interaction plus independent exploration.
- Unmanaged dogs in the environment happen, we can only do our best and move on. As the dog's resilience grows, loose dogs will affect them less.
- Only when the dog is as relaxed outside the home as he is in the home do we move onto systematic desensitisation and counter conditioning.

Summary

*"Histories are more full of examples of
the fidelity of dogs than of friends."*
– Alexander Pope

I hope you have enjoyed the book and learned a lot about your dog and how you can help him to cope in the world. Changing a dog's behaviour is generally always possible, and it's just a case of following effective, careful steps to change how the dog feels – which will automatically change how he reacts.

Remember the following:

1. Evolution matters and so does your dog's prior learning experiences, breed type and personality.
2. Enlightened observation is the key to positive and effective canine communication.
3. Stress and fear are usually the basis of your dog's choices.

4. To change behaviour, we must meet the dog's needs fully and simultaneously remove stress from their lives.
5. Behaviour is based on habitual choices, we can set the environment up to make the better choices easier, to empower the dog. This approach will create new and healthier neural pathways.
6. We only enter behaviour modification when the dog is in a calm state.

This book has explored a lot of factors to behaviour, acknowledging that we must take a holistic approach is key to lasting change. Am empowered dog is a resilient one, and you can empower your dog with consistent care, coaching and positive interactions.

There will be bad days, there always are, but when your dog is resilient, and you can both cope, the bad days will be less and they will affect you both less too.

I want to thank you for reading this, from me and from your dog. We live in a world where the domestic dog is still misunderstood in so many places, but not your dog or mine. So, keep learning, keep focusing on giving your dog the right choices, to build new habits. Best of luck and your dog is lucky to have you!

Glossary of Terms

Aggression. An intent to harm or defensive behaviour display.

Barrier frustration. Aggressive display through a barrier that stops when the barrier is removed.

Chaining. A series of acts that leads to a single result.

Classical Conditioning. Learning from the environment.

Coaching. Teaching through empowerment of the learner.

Continuous Reward. Food reward without a break in delivery, used when teaching a new act or choice.

Coping Threshold. How much stress an individual can take before they are overwhelmed and react.

Cortisol. Stress hormone that occurs when an animal experiences fight or flight.

Counter Conditioning. Changing the response to a specific situation by changing the neural pathway associated with it.

Cue. A word used to prompt a choice or act via a taught link.

Decompression. Allowing stress to dissipate resulting in relaxation.

Dominance. The stronger individual in a situation usually linked to competition for a resource.

Enlightened Observation. Watching and interpreting with accurate knowledge.

Enrichment. Quality time through tasking, that is beneficial to health and wellbeing.

Escape and avoidance learning. The learner changes their behaviour to escape or avoid a situation.

Eustress. Good stress that aids performance.

Flooding. Forcing a learner to be in close proximity to their fears in the hope they will learn to cope.

Left gaze bias. Reading emotional change through micro expressions on the human face.

Long term stress. A continued influx of stress hormone over a long period.

One trial learning. See single event learning – usually occurs when a dog is scared.

Operant Conditioning. Learning from coaching or training.

Reactivity. The tendency to overreact through stress.

Resilience. An inner strength to prevent stress and maintain wellbeing.

Safety bubble. The distance a dog needs around them to feel safe.

Sensitisation. Being sensitive to something specific.

Short term stress. An influx of stress hormone.

Single event learning. Learning from one event.

Social learning. Learning from peers.

Trigger stacking. Exposure to multiple worrying things without a change to recover between them resulting in an overwhelming amount of stress and linked behaviour reaction.

Variable reward. Food reward with breaks in delivery, used when reinforcing a new choice and strengthening the act.

Vicarious learning. A dog learning from other dogs.

Resources

Calming Signals

Stress Yawn   Face Away   Alert

Looking Cute   Submissive   Nose Lick

Cowering   Paw Lift   Play Bow

Head Turn   Butt Sniffing   Ground Sniffing

Fear & Anxiety

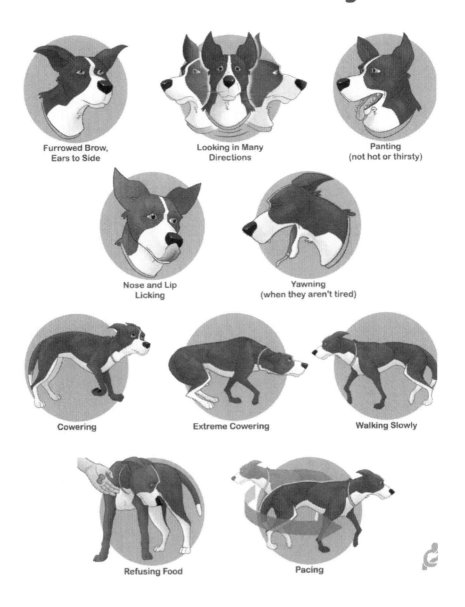

Furrowed Brow,
Ears to Side

Looking in Many
Directions

Panting
(not hot or thirsty)

Nose and Lip
Licking

Yawning
(when they aren't tired)

Cowering

Extreme Cowering

Walking Slowly

Refusing Food

Pacing

Final Note:

If you're reading this through kindle please could you click the star rating at the end of the book. Reviews and ratings are the lifeblood of self-published authors. Reviews dictate readers, readers mean better understood dogs and happier guardians. They also get this work seen by as many people as possible, so I would really appreciate it if you took a moment just to click to share your experience.

Thank you for joining me.

If you have any questions or just want to say hello, you can contact me at my website sallygutteridge.com or info@sallygutteridge.com. I respond to every single message.

Enjoy your dogs!

Made in the USA
San Bernardino, CA
22 January 2020